ANALECTA BIBLICA
INVESTIGATIONES SCIENTIFICAE IN RES BIBLICAS

—— 112 ——

JOHN PAUL HEIL

Kenrick Seminary, St. Louis, Missouri

ROMANS–PAUL'S LETTER OF HOPE

ROME
BIBLICAL INSTITUTE PRESS
1987

ISBN 88-7653-112-2

GREGORIAN UNIVERSITY PRESS
BIBLICAL INSTITUTE PRESS
Piazza della Pilotta, 35 - 00187 Rome, Italy

SIGLA

KNT:	Kommentar zum Neuen Testament
Lev:	Leviticus
LXX:	Septuagint
1 Macc:	First Maccabees
Mal:	Malachi
Matt:	Matthew
MTZ:	Münchener Theologische Zeitschrift
n.:	note
NCB:	New Century Bible
NT:	New Testament
NTS:	New Testament Studies
OT:	Old Testament
p.:	page
Phil:	Philippians
Prov:	Proverbs
Ps:	Psalm
Pss. Sol.:	Psalms of Solomon
RB:	Revue biblique
RGG:	Religion in Geschichte und Gegenwart
RHPR:	Revue d'histoire et de philosophie religieuses
RivB:	Rivista biblica
Rom:	Romans
RSR:	Recherches de science religieuse
SBLDS:	Society of Biblical Literature Dissertation Series
Sir:	Sirach
SJT:	Scottish Journal of Theology
SNTSMS:	Society for New Testament Studies Monograph Series
Str-B:	H. Strack and P. Billerbeck, *Kommentar zum Neuen Testament*
SUNT:	Studien zur Umwelt des Neuen Testaments
TDNT:	G. Kittel and G. Friedrich (Eds.), *Theological Dictionary of the New Testament*
1 Thes:	First Thessalonians
TLZ:	Theologische Literaturzeitung
Tob:	Tobit
v.:	verse
VD:	Verbum Domini
vol.:	volume
Wis:	Wisdom
WMANT:	Wissenschaftliche Monographien zum Alten und Neuen Testament
ZNW:	Zeitschrift für die Neutestamentliche Wissenschaft
ZTK:	Zeitschrift für Theologie und Kirche

TABLE OF CONTENTS

ANALECTA BIBLICA

Romans—Paul's Letter of Hope

John Paul Heil

CHAPTER I

Hope and Romans

A. Introduction

"May the God of hope fill you with complete joy and peace in believing, so that by the power of the Holy Spirit you may abound in hope!" This prayer of Paul to the "God of hope" for an exuberance of hope on the part of his audience occurs at a very strategic point in the letter to the Romans. It brings the main body of the letter (Rom 1:18–15:13) to a hope-filled climax. It thus serves as one of the best of several indications that the theme of hope has been a major concern of Paul throughout the letter. Indeed, a close reading of the entire letter to the Romans discloses an unmistakable tone of hopefulness. The word for "hope" (*elpis*) occurs at several structurally significant places in the letter.[1] And Paul seems to be making a conscious and concerted effort throughout the letter to arouse and increase the hope of his Roman audience. These and other preliminary hints have led us to attempt an in-depth investigation of the theme of hope in Romans. We wish to undertake the following theological-exegetical exploration of Romans not only for the sake of gaining a deeper insight into the important Christian virtue of hope but also for a better understanding of the letter as a unified whole.

The theme of hope is particularly relevant for the situation of the church and mankind in the modern world. There are many phenomena today which can cause widespread feelings of despondency and which indicate the need for a genuine attitude of hope. One example is the threat of total annihilation through nuclear disaster, which has brought some to the pessimism of stockpiling "suicide pills". Other examples include the continual wars throughout the world, the extensiveness of hunger and poverty, environmental and ecological crises, wholesale ethical apathy and moral degradation, the depression and despair of drug, alcohol and sexual abuse, the self-sufficiency and pseudo-security of modern affluence. In view of such a desperate situation with its grim outlook for the future, can Christians really possess a legi-

---

[1] The word *elpis* occurs at the following places in the letter: Rom 4:18; 5:1-5; 8:20; 8:24-25; 12:12; 15:12-13; 15:24. Their structural significance will become evident in the course of our investigation.

timate and authentic attitude of hope? Is there a meaningful and realistic hope that Christians can manifest and offer to the world of today? It is our intention to demonstrate by means of this study that Paul's letter to the Romans presents us with such a hope—a hope that desperately needs to be heard and to become a living reality.

Many authors have recognized that hope is an important theme in Romans.[2] O. Michel has even suggested that "the allusion to "hope" permeates the entire letter to the Romans."[3] In an extensive presentation of the concept of hope K. M. Woschitz has devoted a section to several passages dealing with hope in the letter to the Romans.[4] His study centers on the Greek word *elpis* as a "key-concept" for illustrating many of the significant aspects of the theme of hope in Romans. He does not, however, give a full consideration to the various expressions of hopelessness in the letter, which we think are important for a complete understanding of the meaning and function of hope throughout the letter as a whole. In short, he does not treat the entire letter with all of its many allusions to the concept of hope. G. Nebe has written a book on "hope in Paul," which focuses primarily on the word *elpis* and its synonyms in relation to Paul's eschatology.[5] Like Woschitz, Nebe limits himself to certain words which express the concept of hope. He does not take into account other possible expressions of or allusions to hope. More specifically, he fails to consider not only the opposites

---

[2] There are, of course, many studies which treat the topic of hope in the NT in general or in the Pauline corpus. Some which deal with hope specifically in Romans: J. Lambrecht, "Present World and Christian Hope. A Consideration of Rom. 8: 18-30," *Jeevadhara* 8 (1978) 29-39; M. L. Loane, *The Hope of Glory. An Exposition of The Eighth Chapter in The Epistle to The Romans* (London: Hodder and Stoughton, 1968); A. Maillot, *L'Epître aux Romains, épître de l'espérance. Essai sur le plan de l'Epître aux Romains* (*BVC* 84; Bruges: Desclée De Brouwer, 1968); F. Menezes, "Christian Hope of Glory. Rom 8: 18-30," *Biblebhashyam* 5 (1979) 208-225; J. H. Rische, "'Waiting in Hope': An Exegetical Study of Romans 8: 19-22," A Research Paper Presented to Concordia Seminary, St. Louis, 1970; H. Schlier, "Das, worauf alles wartet. Eine Auslegung von Römer 8,18-30," *Das Ende der Zeit. Exegetische Aufsätze und Vorträge III* (Freiburg/Basel/Wien: Herder, 1971); D. W. B. Robinson, "The Priesthood of Paul in the Gospel of Hope," *Reconciliation and Hope. New Testament Essays on Atonement and Eschatology presented to L. L. Morris on his 60th Birthday* (Ed. R. Banks; Exeter: Paternoster, 1974) 231-245; J. Sudbrack, "Der Hymnus auf die Hoffnung. Eine Einführung in das Verständnis von Röm 8,19-39," *Geist und Leben* 41 (1968) 224-228.

[3] O. Michel, *Der Brief an die Römer* (MeyerK 4; 14th ed.; Göttingen: Vandenhoeck & Ruprecht, 1978) 385.

[4] K. M. Woschitz, *Elpis-Hoffnung. Geschichte, Philosophie, Exegese, Theologie eines Schlüsselbegriffs* (Wien/Freiburg/Basel: Herder, 1979) 497-544.

[5] G. Nebe, *'Hoffnung' bei Paulus. Elpis und ihre Synonyme im Zusammenhang der Eschatologie* (SUNT 16; Göttingen: Vandenhoeck & Ruprecht, 1983).

of hope but also expressions of hope which do not employ an explicit word for "hope".

We endeavor to offer a new and different approach to the topic of hope in Romans. Our study will examine not only the positive concept of hope in itself but the negative counterparts of hope — despair and overconfidence — in their dynamic interaction with hope. Furthermore, our inquiry will seek to demonstrate that there are many expressions and proclamations of hope in Romans which do not use a word for "hope". These considerations will allow us to illustrate the extensiveness of the theme of hope throughout the entire letter. As we will attempt to show, every section of the letter touches upon the theme of hope in one way or another. In sum, our investigation will consider all possible aspects and allusions to "hope" throughout the entire letter in order to demonstrate the full significance of hope in Romans.

B. Method and Preliminary Considerations

With the aid of various theological treatments of hope, we will begin with a basic definition and analysis of the theological elements essential to the dynamics of hope. Then, we will illustrate how these theological elements of hope are indeed present in the letter to the Romans by examining some key passages which contain explicit expressions of hope. We will thus use the most obvious expressions of hope in the letter as a basis for determining the elements of Paul's theology of hope in Romans. Then, by means of these essential theological elements, which are most evident in explicit contexts of hope, we can move to the less obvious expressions of and allusions to hope in the letter. This offers us a sound methodological basis for penetrating the entire letter from the viewpoint of hope.

As for the order of proceeding in the investigation, we prefer to follow the theme of hope precisely as Paul presents and develops it. Therefore, our investigation will follow the letter from beginning to end with respect for what we consider to be the main structural divisions of the document.[6] Following the literary structure of Romans will help us to experience Paul's concerted effort to awaken and increase the hope of his audience.

---

[6] In deciding on how Romans should be structurally divided, we found the following to be helpful: S. Lyonnet, "Note sur le plan de l'épître aux Romains," *RSR* 39 (1951) 301-316; Ph. Rolland, "'Il est notre justice, notre vie, notre salut'. L'ordonnance des thèmes majeurs de l'Epître aux Romains," *Bib* 56 (1975) 394-404; *Epître aux Romains. Texte grec structuré* (Rome: Biblical Institute, 1980); H. Schlier, *Der Römerbrief* (HTKNT 6; Freiburg/Basel/Wien: Herder, 1977) 12-16.

Guided by some basic theological treatments of hope,[7] we can begin with the following rudimentary definition: "Hope" refers to the act or the attitude of confident expectation for God's future salvific activity that arises from faith in what God has promised and/or already accomplished on our behalf. If we carefully analyze this definition, we can detect four essential elements involved in the dynamics of hope: The first element is "what God has promised and/or already accomplished on our behalf." This element might be termed the objective basis or foundation from God for hope. It provides the possibility to hope for God's future salvific activity. This element thus serves as the basis or "promise" for God's further salvific activity or its completion in the future. The second element is "faith". What God has promised and/or accomplished, the objective basis for hope, is recognized, accepted and appropriated through the act or attitude of "faith". The element of faith, then, might be termed the subjective basis or presupposition of hope. And so hope can be considered a consequence of faith. The third element is "the act or the attitude of confident expectation." This element might be termed the subjective expression of hope. It can take the form either of an *attitude* of expectation for God's future salvific activity or of an *act,* that is, a statement, proclamation or expression of hope for the future. The fourth element is "God's future salvific activity." This element might be termed the future object or goal of hope. It expresses that which is hoped for or expected to be brought about by God.

Now we want to show that these essential theological elements of hope are present in the letter to the Romans by examining a couple of key passages containing explicit expressions of hope. Two appropriate passages are Rom 5: 1-11, which contains three occurrences of the word for "hope," *elpis,* and Rom 8: 18-25, which contains six occurrences of *elpis* and several of its synonyms. Together these two passages provide us with a good illustration and confirmation of the above definition of hope.

What we have termed the "objective basis" for hope, "what God has promised and/or already accomplished on our behalf," finds several different modes of expression in these two passages. One of the consequences of our "having been justified" or "made righteous" by God is the fact that we may

---

[7] J. B. Bauer, "Hope," *Sacramentum Verbi* (1st vol.; New York: Herder and Herder, 1970) 376-379; H. Conzelmann, "Hoffnung im NT," *RGG* 3 (1959) 417-418; E. Hoffmann, "Hoffnung," *Theologisches Begriffslexikon zum Neuen Testament* (2d vol.; Wuppertal: Brockhaus, 1969) 722-728; F. Kerstiens, "Hope," *Sacramentum Mundi* (3d vol.; New York: Herder and Herder, 1969) 61-65; J. Macquarrie, *Christian Hope* (New York: Seabury, 1978); K. Rahner, "On the Theology of Hope," *Theological Investigations* (10th vol.; New York: Herder and Herder, 1973) 242-259; H. Schlier, "On Hope," *The Relevance of the New Testament* (New York: Herder and Herder, 1968) 142-155.

"boast of hope for the glory of God" (5 : 1-2).[8] That God has already "justified" us serves as the objective basis or foundation for a "hope" (*elpis*) for the future "glory of God" — a "hope" of which we may even "boast". And the objective basis from God for the statement that this "hope (*elpis*) does not shame" is the fact that "the love of God has been poured out in our hearts through the Holy Spirit who has been given to us" (5 : 5). This "love of God," demonstrated by Christ's death on our behalf (5 : 8), is another way, then, of expressing the objective basis from God for "hope". It assures us that our hope for future salvation from God will not disappoint us or put us to shame. Still another mode of expressing the objective basis for hope can be found in Rom 8 : 23 a: That we already "have the first-fruits of the Spirit" given to us by God forms the foundation for an explicit expression of "hope" in the proclamation that "we have been saved in hope (*elpis*)" (8 : 24 a). Thus, our hope for future salvation from God has an objective basis in God's having already given us of his Spirit. These, then, are some of the different ways that the "objective basis" from God for hope finds expression in the letter to the Romans.

We have termed "faith," as the act of obediently submitting to and subjectively appropriating what God has already done for us, the "subjective basis" for hope. Hope, then, arises from faith (subjective basis) in what God has promised and/or already accomplished on our behalf (objective basis). We can clearly observe this in Rom 5 : 1-2, where the "hope" (*elpis*) of which we boast emerges as one of the consequential benefits of our having been justified "by faith" (*ek pisteōs*). Our faith in what God has already done in justifying us gives us a hope for the future "glory of God". This stands as the only explicit mention of faith as the subjective basis for hope in our chosen passages. There are, however, other places in Romans in which explicit expressions of "hope" are closely associated with and follow upon "faith". In 4 : 18 it was "against hope in hope" (*par' elpidi ep' elpidi*) that Abraham "believed" (*episteusen*) that he would become the father of many nations. Abraham's "faith" in what God had already promised ("Thus will be your seed" (Rom 4 : 18 b; see Gen 15 : 5)) served as the subjective basis for his "hope" to become the father of many nations in the future despite his advanced age and the barrenness of his wife, which militated "against hope". And in 15 : 13 Paul's passionate prayer that his audience abound in "hope" presupposes their "faith": "May the God of *hope* (*elpidos*) fill you with complete joy and peace in *believing* (*pisteuein*), so that by the power of the Holy Spirit you may abound in *hope* (*elpidi*)!" In these examples, then, we see how "hope" is a consequence of "faith," which thus can be called the "subjective basis" for hope.

---

[8] We do not intend to give a full exegesis of these texts. We only want to use them to illustrate the theological elements involved in hope.

The next element in our analysis of the dynamics of hope consists of the various expressions for "hope" itself. Faith in what God has promised or done for us often leads to utterances of hope as the act or attitude of confident expectation for God's future salvific activity. *Elpis* is the usual Greek term for expressing the attitude of "hope". But worthy of note in our chosen passages are the many other terms which seem to be synonymous to or at least used in close conjunction with *elpis*. They help to further describe various dimensions and aspects of the attitude of hope. For example, while boasting of hope in the midst of sufferings, Christians experience that suffering produces "steadfastness," which in turn produces "proven character," which in turn produces more "hope" (*elpida*) (5 : 3-4). Hence, such qualities as "steadfastness" and "proven character" are included in the dynamics of producing and increasing the attitude of hope. They are part of "hope" in the midst of suffering. The intensely forward-looking character of the attitude of hope is emphasized by such terms as "eager expectation" and "await," which describe the "hope" of creation (8 : 18-19) as well as of Christians (8 : 23-25). Patiently striving for God's future salvation in the midst of present sufferings is an aspect of the attitude of hope which finds expression in creation's "groaning together" and "being in travail together" (8 : 22) and in Christians' "groaning within themselves" while "awaiting" future salvation (8 : 23), which they "await" with "steadfastness" (8 : 25).

But of particular importance to our study are the acts or statements of hope which do not employ the term "hope". These kinds of expressions will prove to be helpful as we examine the entire letter under the aspect of hope. A good example of such an expression is found in Rom 5 : 9 b where the proclamation that "we will be saved" from "the wrath" through Christ articulates a hope for future salvation based upon and assured by the fact that "we have now been justified" (5 : 9 a). We may further confirm that "we will be saved" is indeed an expression of hope in this context by comparing the compositional sequence of 5 : 9 with 5 : 1-2: 5 : 9: justified now..... we will be saved..... 5 : 1-2: justified then by faith... we boast of *hope*... In a context of explicit terms for hope (5 : 1-5) "we will be saved" gives expression to and exemplifies the "hope" (*elpis*) of which we boast as well as the "hope" (*elpis*) which does not shame (5 : 5). A parallel example follows immediately in 5 : 10 b which pronounces again the hope that "we will be saved" through the "life" of Christ based upon the fact that we have already been "reconciled" to God through the death of his Son (5 : 10 a). Another excellent example of a future tense verb used to proclaim "hope" occurs in Rom 8 : 20-21. The "in hope" (*eph' helpidi*) aspect of creation having been subjected to futility (8 : 20) is immediately illustrated by the statement of the future hope that creation "will be freed" from the slavery of corruption (8 : 21). Here again a proclamation of future salvation demonstrates the hope that is indicated by the usual expression for "hope," *elpis*.

Dependent upon their content and context, then, similar statements of the future in Romans may serve as expressions of the act of hope.

The final element to be considered in the dynamics of hope consists in the "future object" or goal of hope—God's future salvific activity that is hoped for or expected. There are various ways in which the object of hope finds formulation in our chosen passages. The "glory of God" describes the future goal of the "hope" of which we boast in 5 : 2 b. Other examples of the goal of hope are future salvation from "the wrath" of God and future salvation in the "life" of Christ (5 : 9-10). In 8 : 19-21 the hope of creation is directed toward a future goal formulated as "the revelation of the sons of God" as well as "the freedom of the glory of God's children." We Christians await a future goal of hope in terms of "sonship" and "the redemption of our body" (8 : 23). In 8 : 24-25 we may note that *elpis* itself can be used to refer to that for which we hope. Furthermore, these verses offer us an insight into the character of the future goal of hope: "Now hope (*elpis*) that is seen is not hope (*elpis*). For who hopes (*elpizei*) for what he sees? But if we hope (*elpizomen*) for what we do not see, we eagerly await with steadfastness." Here we observe that "hope" is oriented not to what is presently visible but to the future, invisible, divine realm—in short, the future of God.[9] And so we may infer that the goal of hope, as the yet to be seen future that only God can bring about, remains humanly uncontrollable and incalculable. Hope's ultimate goal, then, is something that will go beyond the sufferings that we presently "see" and experience.

Now that we have illustrated the key elements involved in the theological dynamics of hope, we wish to turn to the opposites of hope. As we have already remarked, we feel it is important to consider the opposites of hope and how they relate to hope in order to better appreciate the significance of the hope that Paul presents in Romans. Since demonstrating the opposites of hope in Romans depends more on the context than on explicit terms, for now we will merely explain in a general way what we mean by the opposites of hope and leave the more detailed analysis to the actual investigation of the letter.

As we will see later in our study, there are two basic opposites or negative counterparts to the positive concept of hope, namely, hopelessness or despair and overconfidence or presumption. Hopelessness or despair refers basically to an absence or lack of authentic hope. We may describe it as the act or attitude in which there can be no expectation for God's future because of the recognition and/or experience of the human condition of sinfulness or separation from God. By overconfidence or presumption, on the other hand, we refer to an act or attitude of confident expectation for the future based

---

[9] See also 2 Cor 4 : 17-18.

upon what one has or thinks he has attained. It can begin with a reliance upon God which deteriorates into a pseudo-reliance when it actually tries to make a claim upon God or God's future. It represents a false security for the future because it is ultimately centered upon oneself.

With these preliminary considerations of hope and its opposites we are ready to begin our inquiry into the theme of hope in Romans. We now invite the reader, then, to join us on our journey through the letter to the Romans in order to experience and appreciate it as Paul's letter of hope.

CHAPTER II

Paul and the Gospel of Hope: Rom 1 : 1-17

A.   Preliminary Hints of Hope

Paul opens the letter by introducing himself and establishing his relationship with his Roman audience. He presents himself as an obedient "slave" of Christ Jesus, called to be an apostle set apart for the gospel of God (1 : 1). It is the gospel about God's Son, Jesus Christ our Lord, who has given Paul an apostolate to bring about the "obedience of faith"[1] among all the nations (1 : 3-5). Since Paul's apostolate extends to *all* nations, it includes the Romans, who are likewise called to belong to Jesus Christ (1 : 6). It is as an apostle of the gospel, then, that Paul greets all those in Rome (1 : 7).

Already in Paul's opening description of the "gospel of God" we note at least some hints that it is a gospel which has to do with hope. Since the gospel fulfills previous promises by God through his prophets in the holy scriptures (1 : 2), it serves as a further "promise" for the continuance of God's salvific activity in the future.[2] As the fulfillment of the hope of past promises, the gospel would naturally awaken new hope for the future. The gospel is about God's Son who not only has fulfilled the prophetic promises for a Davidic messiah (1 : 3) but has already attained the hoped for eschatological life by his resurrection from the dead (1 : 4). Resurrection from the dead was an expectation for the end of time.[3] That God has begun to fulfill this expectation by raising Jesus from the dead and designating him as his Son "with power" (1 : 4) arouses the hope of sharing in his resurrected life and benefitting from his power as Son of God. And so, in this description of the gospel by Paul in traditional, pre-Pauline terms[4] we can detect some preliminary indications of how the gospel serves as a basis for hope.

---

[1] On the various connotations of "obedience of faith" (subjective, objective, epexegetical genitive), see M. Zerwick and M. Grosvenor, *A Grammatical Analysis of the Greek New Testament* (2d vol.; Rome: Biblical Institute, 1979) 457.

[2] E. Käsemann, *Commentary on Romans* (Grand Rapids: Eerdmans, 1980) 9: "... in some sense the gospel, too, retains the character of promise."

[3] Michel (*Römer*, 74) points out how "the resurrection of the dead" is actually an expression of eschatological hope.

[4] Schlier, *Römerbrief*, 23-27.

B. Hope as "Strength" and "Encouragement"

After acknowledging the world-renown faith of the Romans (1 : 8) and communicating his great concern to visit them (1 : 9-10), Paul arrives at the reason he longs to see them: He wants to share some "spiritual gift"[5] with them so that they may be "strengthened" (*stērichthēnai*) (1 : 11). Paul quickly adds that what he has in mind is not a one-way giving on his part but a "mutual encouragement" (*symparaklēthēnai*) through the faith he has in common with the Romans (1 : 12). We feel that these verses (1 : 11-12) disclose an important insight into what Paul intends to accomplish through his letter. As far as his apostolate to the Romans is concerned, Paul does not need to begin by bringing them to the "obedience of faith" (1 : 5), since the faith of the Romans is already well-known (1 : 8). What Paul wishes to do for the Romans, then, is to demonstrate the spiritual benefits they can and should have as a consequence of their faith. He wants them to be "strengthened" and "encouraged" through the faith they already possess and share with Paul (1 : 11-12). And since Paul has been prevented from coming to the Romans and delivering his "spiritual gift" in person, we propose that he intends to do this in the letter itself, a substitute for his personal presence.[6] In other words, we contend that Paul would like the Romans to be strengthened and mutually encouraged with him through his demonstration of the consequences of their faith in the remainder of the letter.

We further propose that the spiritual "strength" and "encouragement" that Paul wants to impart to the Romans through his letter are part of what is meant by "hope". A first indication for this is that, like hope, this spiritual strength and encouragement are consequences of faith. How spiritual strength can be part of the attitude of hope is evident in the spiritual strength that characterizes the hope which accompanies Abraham's faith in Rom 4 : 18-20: "who against hope, in hope believed (18 a). . . and *not weakening* in faith (19 a). . . he did not doubt in disbelief but was *strengthened* in faith" (20 bc). And that "encouragement" can be an aspect of hope is illustrated in Rom 15 : 4-5, where "encouragement" (*paraklēsis*) is one of the attitudes which comes from God to maintain "hope" (*elpida*). Also enlightening is the statement in 2 Cor 1 : 6-7 that the "hope" (*elpis*) of Paul and Timothy for the Corinthians is made firm by their mutual suffering and "encourage-

---

[5] The word *charisma* here does not refer to the more specific, special "gifts" or "charisms" given to individual members of the church, as in 1 Cor 12 : 4-11. Rather, it refers simply to a God-given gift in a general sense. See Schlier, *Römerbrief,* 38.

[6] N. A. Dahl, *Studies in Paul* (Minneapolis: Augsburg, 1977) 77: "Like Paul's other letters, Romans has the characteristics of a genuine letter. It is a written communication between two parties who are spatially separated and is a substitute for personal presence."

ment" (*paraklēsis*). "Strength" and "encouragement" are combined and closely associated with "faith" in 1 Thes 3 : 2: "And we sent Timothy, our brother and co-worker of God in the gospel of Christ, to strengthen (*stērixai*) and encourage (*parakalesai*) you for the sake of your faith." We will attempt throughout our investigation to illustrate further and confirm these indications of how the spiritual strength and encouragement Paul wishes for his audience can be considered part of "hope".

C. The Hope of the Gospel

How will Paul enable the Romans to be strengthened and encouraged through their faith? The mutual faith of Paul and the Romans is faith in the gospel. Paul has his own understanding and insight into the gospel, and this is what he would like to present and share with the Romans in this letter as a substitute for his personal presence. The Romans can be strengthened and mutually encouraged with Paul, then, through their faith in the gospel as presented by Paul. After repeating his inability to visit them despite his many intentions to do so (1 : 13), Paul states his "eager readiness" to "evangelize" those in Rome (1 : 15). He promptly begins to do so by announcing and defining the theme of his letter — the "gospel" of which he is "not ashamed" (1 : 16-17). And as we will now see, it is a gospel of hope.

We have noted that Paul's previous description of the gospel in traditional terms (1 : 3-4) disclosed some hints and implications of how the gospel is a basis for hope. Now, in Paul's more personal description of the gospel in 1 : 16-17 we will see how he makes these implications regarding hope more explicit. As Paul boldly proclaims: "I am not ashamed of the gospel, for it is the power of God for salvation for all who believe, the Jew first and also the Greek. For in it the righteousness of God is revealed from faith to faith, as it is written, 'He who is righteous will live from faith.'"

Let us closely examine this description to observe how the elements of hope are operative in it. Since the gospel is the "power of God" which brings about "salvation," it functions as an objective basis for hope for the future salvific activity of God. The gospel gives this hope for salvation to "all who believe" in it, so that faith serves as the subjective basis for this hope. As the power of God for future salvation, the gospel serves as the basis for Paul's subjective expression of hope in terms of "not being ashamed" of the gospel. Paul's "not being ashamed" expresses his attitude of hope in the gospel as the power of God for present and future eschatological "salvation,"[7] the object or goal of hope.

---

[7] Schlier, *Römerbrief,* 43.

And we can view the dynamics of hope again as Paul completes his description of the gospel in 1 : 17. Since the eschatological "righteousness of God" (*dikaiosynē theou*), God's own relationship of fidelity to his people as their creator and savior,[8] is now revealed in the gospel, it serves as an objective basis for the hope that "he who is righteous will live." The righteousness of God that is now revealed in the gospel is subjectively appropriated within the dimension of faith — "from faith to faith," so that he who is righteous will live "from faith". This hope for eschatological "life," then, has its subjective basis in faith. Believing in the now revealed eschatological righteousness of God, and thus being made "righteous" by faith, gives one the hope promised by the prophet Habakkuk that "he will live." Thus, the future object of this statement of hope is God's eschatological "life," which, as already present[9] for those made righteous by faith, can even now be lived in hope.

We now want to consider the content and significance of the hope expressed in Paul's description of the gospel in 1 : 16-17. Paul declares the hope that the gospel gives him personally in terms of his "not being ashamed" (*ouk epaischynomai*) of the gospel. In the biblical tradition in which Paul stands the idea of "shame" was often applied to one's faith/hope relationship to God. It does not refer so much to the psychological feeling of shame, as to the shame brought about by God.[10] In the OT the idea of "not being shamed" by God is often parallel to "hoping" or "trusting" in him; in other words, that one's "hope" does "not shame" means that it is trustworthy and utterly reliable, since God himself upholds it. Note the following pertinent examples:

LXX Ps 21 : 6 b: Upon you they hoped and were not shamed.
LXX Ps 24 : 2 a: In you I trust, let me not be put to shame.
LXX Ps 24 : 3 a: For all who wait for you, let them not be put to shame.
LXX Ps 24 : 20 b: Let me not be shamed, for I have hoped in you.
LXX Ps 30 : 2 a: In you, Lord, I have hoped, let me never be shamed.

---

[8] For a full treatment of this meaning of "the righteousness of God," see S. Lyonnet, "De "Iustitia Dei" in Epistola ad Romanos," *VD* 25 (1947) 23-34, 118-121, 129-144, 193-203, 257-263; "De notione "iustitiae Dei" apud S. Paulum," *VD* 42 (1964) 121-152; *Les étapes du mystère du Salut selon l'épître aux Romains* (Paris: Cerf, 1969) 25-53; P. Stuhlmacher, *Gerechtigkeit Gottes bei Paulus* (FRLANT 87; Göttingen: Vandenhoeck & Ruprecht, 1965); U. Wilckens, *Der Brief an die Römer* (EKKNT 6/1; Neukirchen-Vluyn: Neukirchener Verlag, 1978) 202-233; S. K. Williams, "The "Righteousness of God" in Romans," *JBL* 99 (1980) 241-290.

[9] Schlier (*Römerbrief*, 46) points out how "he will live" expresses future eschatological life which is already present.

[10] R. Bultmann, "*aischynō*," *TDNT* 1 (1964) 189.

In "not being shamed" of the gospel, then, Paul is proclaiming that the gospel is a completely reliable basis on which to hope for God's salvation.[11] He will not be "shamed" by preaching it to the Romans. Indeed, in sharing his own confident and encouraging confession of hope that his faith in the gospel gives him, we think Paul is already beginning to display and offer the spiritual strength and encouragement he wants to impart to his audience.

The Romans may be spiritually strengthened and mutually encouraged with Paul not only because of his personal display of hope, but because they can have the hope offered by the gospel. As the power of God, the gospel offers a hope for salvation for "*all* who believe" (1 : 16) — thus, for the Romans whose faith is well-known (1 : 8). In addition, the Romans' faith in the "righteousness of God" now revealed in the gospel offers them the hope that they "will live" from this faith that makes them "righteous". Thus, Paul wants the Romans to realize that the faith they share with him (1 : 12) grants them a hope for eschatological "salvation" and "life". In short, Paul wants them to have the hope of the gospel, for this will enable them to be spiritually strengthened and mutually encouraged with him. The gospel that Paul will present by means of his letter, then, is a gospel of hope for the Romans and for all who believe.

D. Paul's "Apostolic Hope"

Before we proceed to see how Paul develops his gospel of hope throughout the letter, we want to mention Paul's own special hope as an apostle. It is the hope Paul has of accomplishing his apostolic task of spreading the gospel of hope, and so we might call it his "apostolic hope". As a hope which is subordinate but oriented to the hope of "all who believe," a consideration of Paul's apostolic hope is important to our study of hope throughout the entire letter. We have already seen several allusions to it: Paul has voiced an ardent, hopeful "longing" to come to the Romans as part of his general spiritual service to God in the gospel of his Son (1 : 9-11). And his intention to come to them that he may achieve some "fruit" among them explains his "eager readiness," his hope, to accomplish his apostolic task of

---

[11] As we will see later, there are other examples of "not being shamed" in relation to hope: Rom 5 : 5; 9 : 33 and 10 : 11. And in Phil 1 : 18c-20 Paul's "not being shamed" consists in his salvation by the support of the Spirit of Christ and is the object of his "eager expectation" and "hope": "Yes, and I shall rejoice. For I know that through your prayer and the support of the Spirit of Jesus Christ this will turn out for my salvation, as it is my eager expectation (*apokaradokian*) and hope (*elpida*) that I shall not be at all ashamed (*aischynthēsomai*), but that with full courage now as always Christ will be honored in my body, whether by life or by death."

bringing them the gospel (1 : 13-15). Thus, Paul has an "apostolic hope" of bringing the gospel of hope to the Romans, that they may have the hope that will strengthen and encourage them (1 : 11-12). We will see further elaboration of Paul's special "apostolic hope" in 15 : 22-33.

E. Summary

To sum up our results, as an apostle for the gospel Paul wants the Romans, whose faith is already world renown (1 : 8), to share with him the hope that accompanies and is a consequence of faith in the gospel. By presenting them with the hope they can have from their faith, Paul will, as we maintain, be fulfilling his desire of imparting to the Romans some spiritual gift that they may be strengthened and mutually encouraged with him through faith (1 : 11-12). We propose, then, that "spiritual strength" and "encouragement" are aspects of the attitude of hope that comes from faith in the gospel. Paul begins to demonstrate and share the hope offered by the gospel by his own encouraging proclamation of hope in terms of "not being ashamed" of the gospel (1 : 16). "Not being ashamed" expresses Paul's hope based on the gospel as the power of God to effect eschatological salvation. The Romans may share with Paul this hope "for salvation," since it is offered to "*all* who believe" (1 : 16). And all who believe in the "righteousness of God" that is now revealed in the gospel may have a hope for eschatological "life" (1 : 17). Thus, as part of his apostolate Paul has an "apostolic hope" to present his gospel to those in Rome (1 : 13-15). It is a gospel which gives Paul the confident hope of "not being ashamed" and which offers the hope for "salvation" and "life" to the Romans and to all who believe. And now, let us see how Paul presents and develops the hope of the "gospel of hope" in his letter to the Romans.

CHAPTER III

From Hopelessness to Hope: Rom 1 : 18–4 : 25

After his spirited announcement of the gospel of hope (1 : 16-17) Paul immediately launches into a discouraging exposition of the horrible hopelessness which imprisons all of humanity (1 : 18-3 : 20). But then Paul shows that there is a new and marvelous hope from the gospel which frees us from our prison of hopelessness (3 : 20-4 : 25).

A. Hopelessness: Rom 1 : 18–3 : 20

Paul methodically demonstrates how everyone is entrapped by one or another mode of hopelessness: He begins by exposing the degradation and utter despair of those who are "ungodly" (1 : 18-32). But even the "godly" cannot escape hopelessness, as Paul surprisingly unmasks the haughty overconfidence of those who consider themselves to be "righteous" (2 : 1-16). And what the "righteous" Jew thinks he may claim as a privileged hope, Paul discloses to be a vain presumption (2 : 17-3 : 8). Whether because of despair or presumption, then, all of humanity is languishing without hope (3 : 9-20).

1. *The utter despair of the ungodly: 1 : 18-32*

Paul commences his demonstration of universal hopelessness by painting a thoroughly bleak picture of the "ungodly" — those who fail to properly acknowledge God as their creator. The entire context and tone is one of hopelessness because of what is in store for the ungodly in the future. As is clear from their presently misguided behavior, all that the ungodly can expect from God in the future is his "wrath" or "anger" (*orgē*), which amounts to their condemnation to final, eschatological punishment.[1] Hence, they have no hope for future salvation from the "wrath of God" (1 : 18). And since the ungodly are well aware of God's just decree that those who act as they

---

[1] G. Stählin, "*orgē*," *TDNT* 5 (1967) 419-447.

do are destined for "death" (1 : 32), they have no hope for future, eschatological "life" from God (1 : 17).

As Paul has asserted, a new, final and definitive salvific activity of God,
the "righteousness of God," is now "revealed" in the gospel for the salvation of all who believe (1 : 16-17). This means that the "wrath of God,"
which had always been experienced throughout history and which was expected to be fully manifested on the day of God's final judgment (see Rom
2 : 5, 8), is now "revealed" with a new, final and decisive quality (1 : 18).[2]
The future, final "wrath of God," then, is already evident in the unrighteous
behavior of the ungodly, who "suppress" the "truth" or "faithfulness" of
God toward humanity,[3] so that their situation before God is now more hopeless than ever. They do not have the hope for future salvation that comes
from recognizing the faithfulness of God.

Paul's poignant commentary of the idolatrous conduct of the ungodly
offers several indications of why they have no hope for God's future. First,
although the eternal deity and power of God is clearly reflected in creation
(1 : 19-20), in their worship of idols the ungodly have failed to honor the true
God (1 : 21). Rather, they have exchanged the glory of the immortal creator
for images resembling mortal creatures (1 : 23), so that they are "without
excuse" before God (1 : 20 b). They have only themselves to blame for their
guilt in failing to acknowledge the true God and thus depriving themselves of
any hope for future salvation from this God. And the hopelessness of the
ungodly is no superficial matter. It is a deep despair which extends to their
inner thoughts — they have become "futile" in their "thinking"; their undis-
cerning mind was darkened (1 : 21); and thinking themselves to be "wise"
they actually became "foolish" in their idolatry (1 : 22).[4]

Another illustration of how the ungodly lack any hope for the future of
God lies in the fact that God himself has "given them up" to the folly of
their ways. How can they have any hope from God when, in response to
their idolatry (1 : 25), it is God himself who "has given them up" (*paredōken
autous*) to impurity in the lusts of their hearts, the dishonoring of their bodies among themselves (1 : 24)? And again, God himself "has given them
up" to dishonorable passions, the dishonoring of one another by unnatural
sexual activity (1 : 26-27). Finally, in response for their not thinking it fit to
acknowledge God, God "has given them up" to an unfit mentality (1 : 28), to
do all kinds of unfitting and thoroughly degrading things (1 : 29-31). If God

---

[2] R. Dabelstein, *Die Beurteilung der 'Heiden' bei Paulus* (Beiträge zur biblischen
Exegese und Theologie 14; Frankfurt/Bern/Cirencester: Lang, 1981) 75.

[3] Dabelstein, *Beurteilung*, 76-77; Schlier, *Römerbrief*, 50-51; Wilckens, *Römer*,
1.104-105.

[4] W. Popkes ("Zum Aufbau und Charakter von Römer 1.18-32," *NTS* 28 (1982)
496) aptly describes the hopelessness evident here.

himself has abandoned them to their own depravity, what hope do they have?[5]

Indeed, the ungodly have locked themselves into a dark dungeon of complete and utter hopelessness. They compound their depravity and despair by not only doing the things they know will condemn themselves to future death, but approving of others who likewise do them (1 : 32 b). Even though they fully know that they are destined to eschatological "death" in accord with God's decree (1 : 32), they persist in their hopeless ways. They possess not the slightest glimmer of hope from God, then, for future eschatological "life" at the last judgment. And so, Paul has effectively established the utter despair of all those who are ungodly and unrighteous.

2. The haughty overconfidence of the "righteous": 2:1-16

Undoubtedly, most of Paul's audience would not place themselves in the category of "ungodly". They would surely abhor such unfitting conduct and be thoroughly disgusted by it. They would judge such wrongdoing as evil and thus not "approve" or condone those who practise it (1 : 32). We may imagine the shock and embarrassment of Paul's audience when he bluntly declares that "you too are without excuse, whoever you are who judge!" (2 : 1 a). Just as the ungodly are "without excuse" before God (1 : 20) and thus have no hope of being saved from God's future and final condemnation, so also "all who judge" them (2 : 1 a). Those who are able to judge evil and who would consider themselves "righteous,"[6] that is, in a "right" relationship with God, likewise have no hope of escaping the condemnation of God (2 : 3 b), since they do the very evil which they judge to be wrong (2 : 1 b-3 a).

Unless they repent, those who judge evil while still doing it are being rather presumptuous of the kindness, patience and forbearance of God (2 : 4). And since they have not yet repented, they are storing up for themselves

---

[5] Popkes ("Römer 1.18-32," 496) points out the human responsibility for the despair inherent in "God's giving them up."

[6] We should not be too quick to equate the "righteous"—"all who judge" (2 : 1 a) with the "Jew". Dabelstein (*Beurteilung*, 64-98) has convincingly argued that in Rom 1 : 18-2 : 16 Paul is not distinguishing between "Gentile" (1 : 18-32) and "Jew" (2 : 1-16) but more broadly between the "ungodly" (including Jews) and the "righteous" (including non-Jews). The special situation of the "Jew" is not directly addressed until Rom 2 : 17.

"wrath" for the day of wrath when God's righteous judgment will be revealed (2 : 5). Hence, their future and final destiny is the same as that of the ungodly — the eschatological "wrath of God" (1 : 18; 2 : 5). Those who consider themselves "righteous," then, are as hopeless as the ungodly.

At the last judgment no one can hope for a special "partiality" from God (2 : 11). God will repay each one strictly in accord with what he does (2 : 6). Only those who do good works may have a hope from God for the future. Those who patiently persevere in the doing of good and seek glory, honor and immortality have an authentic hope, for God will grant them "eternal life" (2 : 7). But those who, out of ambitious self-seeking, disobey the truth and obey unrighteousness have only despair, for they will receive "wrath and fury" (2 : 8). To repeat, everyone who does evil, the Jew first and also the Greek,[7] is destined for distress and anguish in God's judgment (2 : 9); they are without hope for salvation. But everyone who does good, whether Jew or Greek, may hope for future glory, honor and peace from God (2 : 10). The "righteous" who can judge evil yet still do it, then, may not rely upon a privileged partiality toward them from God as a basis for hope.

Paul goes on to illustrate how those "righteous" who rely merely upon hearing or possessing the Law of God would take only a haughty overconfidence rather than a sure hope with them to the future judgment. Of course, those who have sinned "outside the Law" naturally will perish outside the Law (2 : 12 a). But even those who have sinned "under the Law" cannot presume upon any special partiality before God that may come from merely living under or possessing the gift of God's Torah, for they will be judged by God through the Law (2 : 12 b). Such a presumption would amount to a futile overconfidence, not a true hope. Likewise, not mere "hearers" of the Law but only true "doers" of it may have a confident hope that they "will be justified" before God in the judgment (2 : 13). This is further verified in the case of those who do not externally live under or possess the Torah, yet are able to do it from their "hearts," as will become evident on the day of judgment (2 : 14-16).

In sum, those who judge evil yet continue to practise it themselves (2 : 1-11) and who only hear and have the Law but do not practise it (2 : 12-16) can have no sure hope with regard to God's future judgment — only a presumptuous and haughty overconfidence.

---

[7] "The Jew first and also the Greek" (1 : 16; 2 : 9.10) is a traditional, salvation-historical division of humanity which preserves the priority of the Jews. Here it underlines the universality of judgment according to deeds, and does not mean that the "Jew" has been primarily addressed in 2 : 1-11. See Dabelstein, *Beurteilung,* 91-92.

3. *The vain presumption of the Jew: 2 : 17–3 : 8*

Even if those who consider themselves "righteous" can claim no privileged hope in God, what about the righteous Jew? Can not those who are privileged to call themselves "Jew" and who rely upon their celebrated salvation-historical relationship to the Torah given them by God rightly consider themselves to possess an extraordinary hope in God, since they go so far as to "boast"[8] of their unique relationship to God (2 : 17)? Having been instructed in the Law, the Jew is eminently knowledgeable and discerning with regard to the will of God (2 : 18). The Jew is thus placed in a prominent intermediary position between God and the world. God has distinguished the Jew with the privilege and responsibility of making his will known throughout the world. The Jew is confidently convinced that he is to be a guide to the blind, a light to those in darkness (2 : 19), an instructor of the foolish and a teacher of children, since he holds the embodiment of knowledge and truth in the Law (2 : 20). Surely, the Jew has adequate basis for an exceptional hope in God! But alas, the Jew has miserably failed to live up to his prestigious privilege.

Although quite capable of teaching others the Law, the Jew has apparently neglected to teach himself: He preaches against stealing but steals himself; he speaks against committing adultery but commits adultery; he abhors idols but robs temples (2 : 21-22). And so, the Jew who "boasts" of having God's Law as a basis for a special hope in God actually dishonors God by transgressing the very Law of which he "boasts" (2 : 23). The Jews do not exemplify the light and knowledge of God's Law to the world, in accord with their privileged status. Rather than promoting the honor and glory of God's

---

[8] The term for "boast," *kauchaomai,* has the basic meaning of "self-glory" or "take pride in" but with connotations of both "rejoice," "exult," or "praise" as well as "trust," "rely upon," or "have confidence in." It is used with regard to the God-man relation in the OT in both a negative and a positive sense. Negatively it refers to boasting or self-glorying in things other than God; positively, and somewhat paradoxically, to a self-glorying or boasting in God. Jer 9 : 22-23 (LXX) illustrates both uses: "Thus says the Lord: 'Let not the wise man *boast* in his wisdom, let not the mighty man *boast* in his might, let not the rich man *boast* in his riches; but let him who *boasts boast* in this, that he understands and knows that I am the Lord who practises steadfast love, justice, and righteousness on the earth, for in these things is my will, says the Lord.'"

In Romans Paul uses "boasting" in both a negative (2 : 17.23; 3 : 27; 4 : 2) and a positive way (5 : 2-4.11; 15 : 17). In view of justification by faith rather than by works of the Law, the Jewish boasting and reliance upon the Law as a basis for a special hope in God, something originally good in the eyes of the Jews and of Paul, now takes on a pejorative connotation.

name through their unique relationship to the Law, the Jews do precisely the opposite as they fulfill the prophecy of Isaiah 52:5: "The name of God is blasphemed among the Gentiles because of you" (the Jews) (2:24). The exceptional hope or "boast" in God and his Law that Jews may think they can take delight in, then, proves to be nothing more than an arrogant presumption, since they do not do the Law (2:21), although they possess (2:20) and know (2:18) and even teach it (2:19-21).

Paul continues to undermine any special basis for hope the Jews may claim. Circumcision serves as the sign which distinguishes the Jew as a member of God's chosen, covenantal people and thus endows him with the hope of inheriting the salvation God has promised for his people. But circumcision "is useful" or "is of benefit" (ōphelei)[9] for salvation, that is, provides a valid basis for hope in God's future salvation, only if the Jew practises the Law (2:25a). But if the Jew is a transgressor of the Law, his circumcision has become tantamount to uncircumcision (2:25b). Not only that, but if the uncircumcised observe the decrees of the Law, their uncircumcision "will be counted" the same as circumcision by God in the future judgment (2:26). And what is even more astounding, the uncircumcised who carry out the Law by nature "will judge" the Jew who is a transgressor of the law despite having the written letter of the Law as well as circumcision (2:27)! Circumcision grants the Jew who transgresses the Law only a vain presumption.

Why does any hope based upon simply being a Jew or upon the mere external sign of circumcision, without the actual doing of God's Law, amount to an empty and arrogant presumption? Because being a true Jew and being truly circumcised is not simply a matter of outward appearance (2:28). He is a true Jew who is one inwardly, and real circumcision is an interior matter of the heart, inspired by God's spirit rather than the letter of the Law (2:29a). Only these may claim a genuine hope for the eschatological "praise" that is based not on externals so that it comes "from men," but on the spiritual interior so that it comes "from God" (2:29b).[10]

If being a circumcised Jew provides no special hope for God's future salvation, what then is the salvation-historical "advantage" (perisson) of the Jew or the "benefit" (ōpheleia) of circumcision (3:1)? The Jews still have a most important prerogative in God's plan of salvation, for to them have been entrusted "the promises of God" (3:2; see 9:4-5). In that case, is there

---

[9] Michel (Römer, 132) emphasizes how ōphelei here expresses not just an ordinary, general "usefulness" or "benefit," but what is useful or beneficial *for salvation*—that which is effective toward or gives a claim for God's future salvation. As such, then, it expresses an objective basis for hope.

[10] Michel (Römer, 135) points out how "praise" here expresses God's eschatological salvation. As such, then, it represents the object or future goal of hope.

perhaps still a hope for the Jews despite or even through their transgression and unfaithfulness? The attempt to argue this would run as follows: Even if some Jews have been unfaithful, their unfaithfulness will surely not nullify the faithfulness of God (3 : 3). God will be true, even though everyone else be false, as scripture (Ps 50 : 4 b) testifies (3 : 4). If the Jews' unrighteousness actually demonstrates the righteousness of God, then God is surely not unrighteous even in bringing down his wrath when he judges (3 : 5-6). If, therefore, the truth of God abounds to his glory even through the Jews' falsehood, why should they still be condemned as sinners (3 : 7)? By such perverted reasoning the Jews would be entertaining the vain presumption of ultimately escaping condemnation as sinners since their falsehood or sin actually results in God's glory. But this is a futile attempt and a caricature of Paul's position. He is not advocating, as some have accused him, that "we do evil so that good may come" (3 : 8 a). It would be an absurd parody for the Jews to derive an authentic hope based upon their unfaithfulness to God. They make a farce of God's faithfulness and of the seriousness of his wrath, so that "their condemnation is deserved" (3 : 8 b). Despite or even because of their unfaithfulness, then, Jews can claim no extraordinary hope for God's future but only an arrogant and empty presumption.

4. *All are without hope: 3 : 9-20*

Having demonstrated different types of hopelessness, Paul now climactically emphasizes the hopelessness of all: As Paul has just shown (2 : 17-29), in no way do Jews have an "advantage," a special hope for God's salvation (3 : 9 a). On the contrary, "all," both Jews and Greeks, are shackled under the power of sin (3 : 9 b). Since "sin" is experienced as a universal "power" which totally dominates one's existence, determining one's present and future destiny to be the wrath (1 : 18; 2 : 5.8-9; 3 : 5-6) and condemnation (2 : 2-3.5.12; 3 : 5-7) of God,[11] *all* of us are without a hope for future salvation.

Paul graphically illustrates both the universality and the corrupting power of sin with a chain of scriptural quotations in 3 : 10-18. The first quote serves as a summary superscription for the whole chain: "There is no one righteous, no, not one" (3 : 10). Since hope for God's future salvation is based upon being "righteous" before God (2 : 13; 1 : 17 b), that "no one is righteous" announces the basis for universal hopelessness. And the rest of the chain of quotes further describes why *all* are without hope: "*no one understands*" (3 : 11 a); "*no one* seeks God" (3 : 11 b); "*all* have turned aside

---

[11] Käsemann, *Romans*, 86: "The reality of the world is determined by being subject to this power and hence delivered up to God's wrath."

(from God), together they have gone wrong" (3 : 12a); "*no one* does good" (3 : 12b); and "there is no fear of God before their eyes" (3 : 18). The deadly power of sin (3 : 13-15) condemns everyone to a hopeless future of "ruin and misery" (3 : 16).

Paul then climaxes the utter hopelessness of the ungodly (1 : 18-32), the haughty overconfidence of the righteous (2 : 1-16) and the arrogant presumption of the "righteous" Jew (2 : 17 – 3 : 8) : Whatever the Law says applies to all those who live within the realm of the Law, so that "*every mouth*" may be stopped and "*the whole world*" may be held accountable to God (3 : 19). For "*no human being*" can hope that he "will be justified" before God by the works of the Law, for through the Law comes knowledge of sin (3 : 20). Only the doers of the Law can have the hope that they "will be justified" before God (2 : 13) in the final judgment (2 : 16). But there is not one human being who is righteous (3 : 10), not one doer of the Law (3 : 9-19), so that no human being has any basis whatsoever for the hope of being justified before God (3 : 20). Because there is no one who does the works of the Law, the Law can offer no hope but simply helps us to recognize and experience the hopeless power of sin, so that we are made even more aware of our hopelessness before God. And so Paul has established the total hopelessness of all of humanity (1 : 18-3 : 20). [12]

B. Hope : Rom 3 : 21 - 4 : 25

Although the all-pervasive power of sin has robbed the Law of any power to provide hope, there is yet a remedy for this horrible situation of universal hopelessness. Paul indicates how there is still a basis for hope, a hope offered to all who are now justified by faith rather than by works of the Law (3 : 21-31). This hope can eliminate forever the dire hopelessness of all of humanity. And Paul cogently portrays this hope that now comes apart from the Law by pointing to the important figure of Abraham, our father not only in faith but in hope (4 : 1-25).

1. *Hope for all apart from the Law : 3 : 21-31*

Paul voices again the wretchedness of our universal hopelessness : Since *all* have sinned, all are presently lacking of the "glory of God" (3 : 23), and

---

[12] Käsemann, *Romans,* 89: "This part of the letter ends, then, with a statement of general hopelessness." And on p. 90: "That with the law nothing else is provided is the decisive point. For thus it is shown that even the way of the pious is hopeless prior to and apart from Christ."

hence have no basis to hope for the future "glory of God" (2 : 7.10; 5 : 2 b; 8 : 18). But now that the "righteousness of God" is manifested apart from the Law (3 : 21 a), there is a firm foundation for a new hope for the "glory of God". Although independent of the Law, this "righteousness of God" is attested by the Law and the Prophets (3 : 21 b). As the fulfillment and continuation of the salvific activity previously promised by God's scriptures, then, this newly manifested "righteousness of God" naturally arouses a new hope in God. It is a new hope based not on the works of the Law but on faith, as this "righteousness of God" is now appropriated through faith in Jesus Christ (3 : 22 a). Faith, then, serves as the subjective basis for this new hope, which can offset the hopelessness of *all*, since the "righteousness of God" is offered to "*all* who believe" (3 : 22 a).

So, although *all* have sinned, there is still hope! All who have sinned are now "justified" as a gracious gift of God through the redemption which is in Christ Jesus (3 : 24). That God put forth Jesus as an expiation for sin demonstrates the "righteousness of God" through his forgiveness of past sins, so that God himself is "just" as he "justifies" all who now live from faith in Jesus (3 : 25-26). Since God now forgives and "justifies" all sinners through faith, they may once again hope for the future "glory of God" (3 : 23). This new and wonderful hope for all who are justified by God through faith, then, counteracts and conquers the utter hopelessness of all who have sinned (1 : 18– 3 : 20.23).

What then becomes of the Jewish "boasting" in God (2 : 17) or in the Law (2 : 23), which Paul has already shown to be an arrogant presumption (2 : 21-24)? It is now totally eliminated by the "Law of faith," for now one is justified before God by faith apart from works of the Law (3 : 27-28). The new hope which excludes the old "boasting" arises from faith, not works of the Law. Furthermore, the Jews should not presume, just because they are Jews and have been given the Law, that they are entitled to any kind of special hope in God. For God is surely not the God of the Jews only; no, he is the God of the Gentiles as well (3 : 29). Inasmuch as God is one, then, all, both Jews and Greeks, may have one and the same hope that the one God "will justify" both the circumcised (Jews) and the uncircumcised (Gentiles) through faith (3 : 30). And rather than nullifying or invalidating the Law, the faith that gives rise to this new hope actually upholds and validates the Law (3 : 31), restoring it as the gift of God's instruction and the power of his salvific will.[13] Thus, there is a unity and universality to the new hope that comes from justification by faith rather than works of the Law—it is *one and the same* hope for *all* who believe.

---

[13] Schlier, *Römerbrief*, 119-120.

2. *Abraham, our father in faith and hope: 4 : 1-25*

Descent from Abraham[14] was the pride of every Jew, and we have evidence of a Jewish hope of avoiding God's eschatological "wrath" based simply upon physical descent from Abraham.[15]   We also know of Jewish traditions that Abraham observed the entire Law even before it was written so that he was indeed "justified" before God.[16]   May not the Jews as the children of Abraham "according to the flesh" (4 : 1), then, claim a privileged hope in God on account of the "boasting" which Abraham, their forefather, has from being justified by doing the works of the law (4 : 2 a)?

Paul bluntly dismisses any such claim by explaining that if Abraham has reason to boast "before God" (4 : 2), it is because he has been justified by *faith*, not by *works* of the Law.   As scripture verifies : "Abraham *believed* God, and it was reckoned to him as righteousness" (Gen 15 : 6 in Rom 4 : 3). Abraham's "faith" should not be interpreted as another "work" of the Law or as his "faithfulness" in observing the Law.[17]   Rather, it is a radical and humble trust of one who "does no work," but "believes" in the "One who justifies" the ungodly (4 : 5 a).   Abraham's faith thus includes the recognition that he is "ungodly" (*asebē*), and as such hopelessly doomed for the "wrath of God" (1 : 18).   This is the faith that God reckons as righteousness (4 : 5 b), "according to grace" and not "according to the debt" of one who does work (4 : 4).   And such faith brings with it an authentic hope in God.

---

[14] On the figure of Abraham in Rom 4, and the extent to which Paul differs from Jewish interpretations, see K. Berger, "Abraham in den paulinischen Hauptbriefen," *MTZ* 17 (1966) 47-89, esp. 63-77; Ch. Dietzfelbinger, *Paulus und das Alte Testament. Die Hermeneutik des Paulus, untersucht an seiner Deutung der Gestalt Abrahams* (Theologische Existenz Heute 95; Munich: Kaiser, 1961); E. Jacob, "Abraham et sa signification pour la foi chrétienne," *RHPR* 42 (1962) 148-156; E. Käsemann, "The Faith of Abraham in Romans 4," *Perspectives on Paul* (London: SCM, 1971) 79-101; G. Mayer, "Aspekte des Abrahambildes in der hellenistisch-jüdischen Literatur," *EvT* 32 (1972) 118-127.

With regard to the debate about the "typological" interpretation of Abraham (see L. Goppelt, "Apokalyptik und Typologie bei Paulus," *TLZ* 89 (1964) 321-344), we would like to point out that Paul himself does not use the term "type" for Abraham. (He does use it for Adam (*typos*) in Rom 5 : 14).   Rather, he refers to Abraham as "forefather" (4 : 1) or "father" (4 : 11.12.16.17.18), indicating that justification by faith is not only typified or exemplified by Abraham, but that it originated with him.

[15] Matt 3 : 7-9; Luke 3 : 7-8; John 8 : 32-59; Joachim Jeremias, *"Abraam,"* TDNT 1 (1964) 8-9.

[16] Sir 44 : 20; *Jub.* 23 : 10 a; C. T. Rhyne, *Faith Establishes the Law* (SBLDS 55; Chico: Scholars Press, 1981) 78, 157-158 n. 80; Jeremias, *"Abraam,"* 8.

[17] 1 Macc 2 : 52; Jas 2 : 21-23; Rhyne, *Faith,* 79; Schlier, *Römerbrief,* 123-124.

In a "makarism," a prophetic promise of salvation[18] uttered by David (Ps 32 : 1-2), Paul begins to describe the hope which accompanies Abraham's faith (4 : 6).[19]   It is a hope for the forgiveness of sins, a hope presently experienced as a joyful, God-given "blessedness" not only because of the *assurance* that past sins have been forgiven by God (4 : 7), but because of the hope for God's future, eschatological forgiveness as well.   The future dimension of this hope is emphatically expressed in the climax of the makarism : "Blessed is the man whose sin the Lord *will never reckon (ou mē logisētai)*" (4 : 8).[20]   Abraham's faith, then, brings a sure and blessed hope for God's forgiveness, a hope which offers a replacement for the miserable hopelessness caused by the deadly power of sin (1 : 18 – 3 : 20.23).

Furthermore, this blessed hope for the forgiveness of sins (4 : 6-8) is available not just to circumcised Jews, but to all who believe as Abraham did.   As Paul persuasively asserts, Abraham was justified by God while he was yet uncircumcised (4 : 9-10),[21] so that circumcision was not a necessary condition for his justification.   Circumcision served only as a "sign," a "seal" of the righteousness of faith which Abraham received while yet uncircumcised, so that he is the father of all who believe without being circumcised (4 : 11).   The hope which comes from Abraham's faith, then, extends also to his uncircumcised children who believe in God as he did.   Abraham remains the father of the circumcised as well, but their participation in the hope of Abraham depends upon likewise following in the footsteps of the faith which Abraham had before being circumcised (4 : 12).   Hence, the hope for the forgiveness of sins that comes from Abraham's justification by faith (4 : 6-9) is a hope open to all (3 : 29-30), based not on mere physical descent

---

[18] F. Hauck, "*makarios*," *TDNT* 4 (1967) 369: "the blessing of salvation in special measure"; Käsemann, *Romans,* 113: "prophetic promise of salvation"; Schlier, *Römerbrief,* 125: "ein Heilszuspruch".

[19] In Rom 4 : 6-8 Paul links a Prophets text from Ps 32 : 1-2 to the previous Torah text from Gen 15 : 6 (4 : 3) by means of the Jewish exegetical method known as *gᵉzērāh shāwāh*.   It is the second exegetical rule of Rabbi Hillel and consists of the mutual interpretation of two scriptural passages, which can be associated to one another through a term they have in common (see H. L. Strack, *Einleitung in Talmud und Midrasch* (6th ed.; Munich: Beck, 1976), 97).   In this case the common term is "reckon" (*elogisthē* in Gen 15 : 6 and *logisētai* in LXX Ps 31 : 1-2).

[20] On this emphatic negative expression for the future, see M. Zerwick, *Biblical Greek* (4th ed.; Rome: Biblical Institute, 1963) 149-150; C. E. B. Cranfield, *A Critical and Exegetical Commentary on the Epistle to the Romans* (ICC; 2 vols.; Edinburgh: T. & T. Clark, 1975, 1979) 234: "*ou mē logisētai* is emphatic: 'will in no wise reckon'."; Schlier, *Römerbrief,* 120: "... nimmermehr anrechnet."

[21] According to Jewish rabbinic tradition Abraham was circumcised (Gen 17 : 10-11) 29 years after the establishment of the covenant in Gen 15 : 10.   See Str-B, 3.203.

from Abraham (4 : 1), but on the spiritual descent which consists in imitating the faith of "our father Abraham" (4 : 11-12).[22]

Paul proceeds to illuminate the hope for God's future eschatological salvation that is based on the powerful "promise"[23] to Abraham and his descendants,[24] a "promise" of being an "heir" to the future, final "world" of God's making.[25] As Paul insists, this hope-bringing promise of God is rendered operative and effective as a basis for hope through justification by faith not "through the Law" (4 : 13). Wherever the Law is operative "transgression" results, so that the power of the Law for the future resides in its producing the "wrath" of God (4 : 15), the future object not of hope but of hopelessness (1 : 18; 2 : 5.8; 3 : 5). If those who live under the power of the Law would be heirs to God's future, then faith would be emptied of its significance and the promise would be "nullified" or rendered powerless as a basis for the hope of inheriting God's future salvation (4 : 14). Therefore, the hope of being an "heir" to God's future must come "from faith," so that the promise can remain a valid and powerful basis of hope for *all* the descendants of Abraham, not just for those who have the Law but for those who share the faith of Abraham, the father of us all (4 : 16).

---

[22] Jeremias, "*Abraam*," 9: "The decisive thing is no longer physical but spiritual descent."

[23] Although there are various "promises" by God to Abraham in the the OT (e.g., that Sarah would give birth to Isaac (Gen 15 : 4; 17 : 16, 19); the possession of the land of Canaan (Gen 12 : 1.4; 13 : 14.15.17; 15 : 7.18-21; 17 : 8); countless descendants (Gen 12 : 2; 13 : 16; 15 : 1-3; 17 : 5-6; 18 : 18; 22 : 17); blessing for all peoples of the earth (Gen 12 : 2-3; 18 : 18), Paul is not as interested here in the *content* of the individual promises as he is in the *fact* of the promise as the powerful word of God for the future. See Dietzfelbinger, *Paulus und das AT*, 7; Schlier, *Römerbrief*, 129.

[24] The "or" (*ē*) in the phrase "to Abraham *or* to his seed" is the correlative or copulative *ē*, which thus signifies that with regard to the promise there is no difference between Abraham and his descendants, the promise of being "heir to the world" holds for both. See BDF, § 446; Schlier, *Römerbrief*, 129.

[25] For Paul, as for several other writers from the same apocalyptic-eschatological milieu, "the promise" to Abraham and his descendants refers to God's promise of future eschatological salvation. See, for example, *2 Apoc. Bar.* 14 : 13; 51 : 3; 57 : 1-3; 4 Ezra 7 : 119; Sir 44 : 21.

"World" expresses future eschatological salvation in *2 Apoc. Bar.* 14 : 13: "... and trusting with joy they hope to receive the world which Thou hast promised them" (*APOT*, 491); 51 : 3: "... that they may be able to acquire and receive the world which does not die, which is then promised to them" (*APOT*, 508); see also 57 : 1-3.

The idea of the promise to Abraham in terms of the "inheritance" of the world occurs in Sir 44 : 21. W. Foerster ("*klēronomos*," *TDNT* 3 (1965) 785), in reference to Rom 4 : 13, says: "Here too, where it refers back to the OT, *klēronomos* has an eschatological content."

How Abraham became our father shows us the kind of hope that accompanies faith in God's powerful promise for the future. God promised Abraham that "I have made you the father of many (*pollōn* = "all")[26] nations" (Gen 17 : 5 b). Abraham responded by believing in the God "who gives life to the dead and calls the things that do not exist into existence" (4 : 17).[27] In other words, Abraham humbly trusted that the creative and salvific power of God was great enough to fulfill such a seemingly ridiculous promise. Indeed, it was "against hope in hope" that Abraham believed he would become the father of all nations, according to God's powerful promise (Gen 15 : 5 b) that "thus will be your descendants" (4 : 18).

Here we perceive a definite contradictory tension in the hopeful faith of Abraham. The peculiar phrase "against hope in hope" (*par' elpida ep' elpida*) exemplifies the dramatic rhetorical device known as oxymoron, the combination of contradictory concepts into a unity, preserving a strong tension of contradiction.[28] The contradictory tension in the faith of Abraham lies in the combination of his weak human condition with the powerful promise of God. The "against hope" aspect of Abraham's faith has already been hinted in the words "the dead" and "the things that do not exist" (4 : 17 b). This is Abraham's situation "against hope"—he is as good as "dead" (4 : 19) and his descendants "do not yet exist." Likewise the "in hope" aspect of Abraham's faith has already been foreshadowed in the description of the God who "gives life" and "creates" (4 : 17b). It is the salvific and creative power of God that enables Abraham to believe "in hope". And so the decisive emphasis within the tension of this oxymoron falls upon the "in hope" aspect. Abraham's faith in the power of God is a faith "in hope" despite his "against hope" situation. But precisely how does Abraham's hope predominate over his hopelessness to give him an ultimately "hopeful" faith? What kind of hope emerges from Abraham's struggle to resolve the contradiction within his faith?

As Paul elaborates, Abraham "did not weaken in faith." He thus continued to believe in the power of God, even when he considered the hopelessness of his own "deadened" body and the "deadness" of his wife's womb (4 : 19).[29] This underscores for us the honest realism of his hope. Far from

---

[26] "Many" (*pollōn*) here is the Semitic inclusive or universal "many" which is equivalent to "all"; Joachim Jeremias, "*polloi*," *TDNT* 6 (1968) 536-545.

[27] For the traditional OT and Jewish background to this divine predication in 4 : 17 b, see O. Hofius, "Eine altjüdische Parallele zu Röm. iv. 17 b," *NTS* 18 (1971-72) 93-94.

[28] H. Lausberg, *Handbuch der Literarischen Rhetorik* (2 d ed.; Munich: Hueber, 1973) § 807.

[29] For 4 : 19 the variant readings "he considered" (*katenoēsen*) rather than "he did *not* consider" (*ou katenoēsen*) and "already" (*ēdē*) are accepted here. For the reasons,

being an illusion, a dream, or a mere wish, the hope of Abraham includes a full recognition that his human condition stands in direct contradiction to the promise of God. With a "deadened" (*nenekrōmenon*) body too old to father a child and with the "deadness" (*nekrōsin*) of the aged womb of Sarah (Gen 17:17) Abraham's weak human condition confronts the power of the God in whom Abraham believes, the God who gives life to the "dead" (*nekrous*, 4:17:b). But precisely this life-giving power of God resolves the contradiction that Abraham's weak, "deadened" condition presents to the promise of God. And so, it is "in view of" or "on account of"[30] the powerful promise of God that Abraham "did not doubt in disbelief but was strengthened in faith" (4:20).

That Abraham "did not doubt in disbelief" shows us the "temptation" aspect to Abraham's hopeful faith. "Disbelief" (*apistia*) means more than a mere absence of faith; it means a denial of faith in God, which here would include a rejection of the promise given Abraham by God. "Doubt" (*diakrinesthai*) designates an uncertain wavering or hesitating within oneself between two possibilities. The two possibilities for Abraham are, on the one hand, his "deadened" state (4:19b), his "against hope" situation, which presents him with the possibility of denying his faith and rejecting the promise; and, on the other hand, "the promise of God" (4:20a), the basis for Abraham to believe "in hope". Not only did Abraham's faith in God's powerful promise enable him to overcome the temptation to doubt in disbelief, but his faith actually gained strength precisely in and through the struggle of the temptation (4:20c). In fact, the temptation seems to result in Abraham's faith being strengthened even beyond the overcoming of the temptation.[31] Thus, the "in hope" aspect of Abraham's faith includes a dramatic "strengthening" by the power of God's promise amid the tempting inclination to despair.

As an elaboration of his being strengthened in faith by the promise of God, Abraham "gives glory to God" (4:20d).[32] In the context this denotes that he acknowledged God's "power" or "glory" by permitting that power to

---

see B. M. Metzger, *A Textual Commentary on the Greek New Testament* (London/New York: United Bible Societies, 1971) 510-511.

[30] Zerwick, *Biblical Greek*, 32; A. Oepke, "*eis*," *TDNT* 2 (1964) 427; BAGD, 230; J. R. Mantey, "The Causal Use of *Eis* in the New Testament," *JBL* 70 (1951) 46-47.

[31] The positive and more satisfactory formulation, "was strengthened in faith," is emphatically heightened by the rhetorical process of "correct i o" (Lausberg, *Rhetorik*, § 784-785), as it "corrects" the negative and less satisfactory formulation, "did not doubt in disbelief."

[32] "To give glory to God" is a fixed biblical expression, which refers not to giving God something he does not already have, but to an active acknowledgment of God's divine mode of being, his splendor or power. See G. Kittel, "*dokeō*," *TDNT* 2 (1964) 247-248. On the biblical and Jewish background, see pp. 242-247, esp. 244; Schlier, *Römerbrief*, 134.

be activated for him through his faith in God's powerful promise.[33] Abraham thus allowed God to be God, he allowed the divine power to operate within him, and so God was thereby "given glory" or "glorified". To the "in hope" (4:18 a), "strengthened" (4:20 c) aspect of Abraham's faith in God we may add his "giving glory to God" (4:20 d), his active acknowledgment and honoring of God's power.

Paul not only climactically concludes his explanation of Abraham's "strengthening in faith" (4:20 c), but succinctly sums up his entire description of Abraham's hope (4:17 b-21) on the note that Abraham was "fully convinced" that what God had promised God was capable also to accomplish (4:21). "Fully convinced" (*plērophorētheis*) is a particularly strong expression, meaning to be "fully and completely taken up and convinced."[34] Abraham's complete certainty corresponds to his not doubting, hesitating or wavering in uncertainty (4.20 b) between his hopeless situation and the powerful promise of God (4:19-20 a). Abraham's "complete conviction" thus expresses the complete confidence and absolute certainty that are part of authentic hope. The future object of Abraham's "full conviction" is that God has the power to accomplish what he has promised (4:21 b). In other words, Abraham is fully convinced of the future completion of God's salvific activity. The "promise" of God to Abraham and his descendants (4:13.16) is God's word (4:18 b) about his future salvation. And the basis for the future fulfillment of God's promised salvation is the "power" (*dynatos*) of God (4:17 b.21 b).[35] This power not only guarantees the *future* completion of the promised salvation, but fills Abraham with a *present* attitude of sure hope, a "complete conviction" about the God of the future.

As we can see in his prolonged description of Abraham's faith, Paul is clearly interested in more than the mere fact that Abraham "believed" in Gen 15:6 a. He draws out the implications and consequences of that faith by illustrating various aspects of the attitude of hope which accompanied it. For Paul, this is the kind of faith — a "fully convinced" (4:21 a), "strengthened" (4:20 c), "against hope in hope" (4:18 a) faith — which God reckoned to Abraham as righteousness in Gen 15:6 b (4:22). Paul thus highlights Abraham's attitude of hope as a consequence and essential part of his faith.

Paul explicitly relates his interpretation of the faith of Abraham to "us" (4:24 a), that is, to Paul and his fellow Christians, including those in Rome.

---

[33] On "glory" as the "power" of God, see Kittel, "*dokeō*," 243-248.

[34] Schlier, *Römerbrief*, 135; G. Delling, "*plērophoreō*," *TDNT* 6 (1968) 309-310.

[35] On 4:21 Delling ("*plērophoreō*," 310) says: "Abraham's faith is completely certain of the full agreement between God's promise and His power, which can call into being things which are not, awaken what is dead to life, and give Abraham a posterity."

He indicates that what was written in the scriptures about the promise for Abraham, also "was written" and applies "for us" (4 : 23).[36] In other words, since the promise to Abraham and his descendants is through the "righteousness of faith" (4 : 13), then this same promise for God's future, final salvation is also "for us to whom it will be reckoned (as righteousness)" (4 : 24 a)[37] and who believe in the God who raised Jesus for our "justification" (4 : 25 b). Thus, the promise, which was valid for Abraham's faith, holds valid also for us who believe like Abraham (4 : 16). And the validity of the promise entails not only the certainty of its future fulfillment but also its power in the present, as evident in the hope it added to Abraham's faith (4 : 18-21). Just as Abraham's faith was oriented to the future completion of God's salvific activity and thus entailed a present attitude of hope, so also "for us" Christians and our faith. Paul implies that "for us" who believe in the same God as Abraham did, the God of power and the promise, there is also for our faith a present attitude of hope for God's future, final salvation based on the salvific death and resurrection of Jesus (4 : 24 b-25). At this point, then, through the very strong implications which the hopeful faith of our father Abraham carries for the hopefulness of our faith, Paul is arousing and leading "us" to Christian hope, which he will begin to explain and describe in 5 : 1-11.[38]

As we earlier proposed, one of Paul's purposes for sending his letter is that his Roman audience might be "strengthened" and "mutually encouraged" through the faith they share with Paul (1 : 11-12). We likewise proposed that "strength" and "encouragement" in faith describe attributes of hope, so that Paul intends his letter to contribute to the hope of his fellow Christians in Rome. With his dramatic illustration of the "in hope" faith of Abraham, a faith which Paul and his fellow Christians share with Abraham, "our father," we see how Paul is achieving his goal of arousing hope. Just as the hopeful faith of Abraham included his being "strengthened" in faith, so also Paul and his audience, who share the same faith, may likewise be

---

[36] See Rom 15 : 3-4; 1 Cor 9 : 9-10; 10 : 11; Schlier, *Römerbrief,* 135.

[37] The word *mellei* here denotes "an action that necessarily follows a divine decree" (BAGD, 501): "is destined," "must," "will certainly". It thus refers to a future event which is certain from divine necessity. Although the expression "it will be reckoned" (*mellei logizesthai*) here refers to the eschatological future "reckoning as righteousness," or "justification," it implies and presupposes the present justification of Christians who believe (see, for example, 1 : 16-17; 3 : 21-28; 4 : 25 b; 5 : 1 a). Schlier, *Römerbrief,* 135.

[38] As Delling ("*plērophoreō*," 310) states: "Because the faith of Abraham in R. 4 is a model for the faith of Christians, justifying faith, based on confidence in God's promise and creative power, is a faith which is "fully certain" of God's act, a faith in the new life which is given to the Christian in justification."

"strengthened" and "mutually encouraged" in their faith, that is, they may manifest the spiritual strength and encouragement of hope.

Paul began to carry out his purpose of awakening the hope of his fellow Christians when he announced the theme of the letter with his own confident confession of hope (1 : 16-17). Paul's own hope parallels that of Abraham and exhibits the same basic structure: First, that Abraham's hope is oriented to God's salvific activity as expressed by the "promise" (4 : 13,14.16.20-21) corresponds to Paul's hope being oriented to God's salvific activity as expressed by the "gospel" (1 : 1,9.15-16).[39] Second, just as Abraham's hope for the future fulfillment of God's promise rests upon the "power" of God (4 : 17 b) as the one who is capable (*dynatos*, 4 : 21) of accomplishing what he has promised, so also Paul's hope rests upon the gospel as the "power" (*dynamis*, 1 : 16 b) of God for salvation. Third, the promise which filled Abraham with hope extends to "all" (4 : 16) the descendants who share the faith of Abraham so that they may have hope, like Abraham. And the gospel which fills Paul with hope is God's power for the salvation of "all who believe" (1 : 16 b) and thus share the faith of Paul, so that they may likewise share his hope. Fourth, Abraham's being "fully convinced" (4 : 21 a), which underlines the confidence and certainty of his hope, is similar to Paul's confident hope of "not being ashamed" (1 : 16 a) of the gospel. So, after Paul has displayed his own confident hope to those to whom he is writing the letter (1 : 8-17), he bolsters this display by adding to it his eloquent description of Abraham's hope (4 : 13-25). Abraham believed and had hope; Paul believed and had hope; Paul's fellow Christians, including those in Rome, who believe like Abraham (4 : 16.24 a) and like Paul (1 : 8.12.16 b), may likewise have hope.

C. Summary

Having investigated the theme of hope in Rom 1 : 18 – 4 : 25, we may set forth the following results:

1) Paul has effectively and emphatically established that in one way or another all of humanity is entangled and entrapped in the dreaded doom of hopelessnes (1 : 18 – 3 : 20). The ungodly, unrighteous display a thoroughly death-bringing despair (1 : 18-32); the so-called "righteous" exhibit only a haughty overconfidence (2 : 1-16); and the Jews can claim no special hope in God based on the Law (2 : 17-24) or circumcision (2 : 25-29) or a presumption of God's faithfulness (3 : 1-8) despite their transgression of the Law. *All*

---

[39] In Rom 1 : 2 the "gospel" was "promised beforehand" through the prophets in the holy scriptures.

have in fact sinned and transgressed the Law of God, and so no one can cling to even the slightest glimmer of hope before God (3 : 9-20,23).

2) But now the "righteousness of God" offers us all a wonderfully new hope independent of the Law. This new hope comes through the death of Christ which brings us the forgiveness of our sins, the needed remedy for the miserable hopelessness which overwhelms all who have sinned (3 : 21-31). So, all who are now justified by believing in God may now overcome and replace their wretched hopelessness with a new, authentic and living hope in God.

3) Abraham, the father of all who believe, dramatically illustrates some of the important attributes of the hope that fills one who is justified by faith. His hope included the joyful "blessedness" of present and future forgiveness of sins (4 : 3-8); the confidently "full conviction" in God's power to accomplish the future salvation he had promised (4 : 21); and a spiritual "strengthening" in faith aroused by the power of God's promise, which enabled him to believe "in hope" despite the inclination to disbelief presented by his human condition, which was entirely "against hope" (4 : 18 a). Abraham modeled a completely realistic hope, then, taking into full consideration the contradiction which his weak, human situation presented for the future fulfillment of God's promise (4 : 18-20).

4) Paul's vivid presentation of Abraham's bold and confident hope promotes his purpose of arousing hope in his audience (1 : 11-12). The Romans and all Christians, who share the faith of Paul (1 : 8.12.16 b) and of Abraham (4 : .16.24 a), may likewise share in the exuberant hope of Paul (1 : 16 a) and of Abraham (4 : 13-25).

CHAPTER IV

The Hope of Christians: Rom 5 : 1 – 8 : 39

With the strong and sure hope of our father Abraham as his springboard, Paul leaps into an eloquent exposé of Christian hope in this key section of the letter (Rom 5 – 8). He enthusiastically announces the tremendously reliable and realistic hope he and his fellow Christians may joyfully proclaim (5 : 1-11). This new and gracious hope far surpasses the deadly doom and gloom of our old hopelessness (5 : 12-21). We Christians can already begin to live the splendid future life for which we hope (6 : 1-14). In fact, it is urgently imperative for us to live now this new and marvelous life of hope (6 : 15-23). For ours is a hope which liberates us from the dreaded despair (7 : 1-6) produced by the "Law" of sin and death (7 : 7-25). Now we Christians live under the new "Law" of God's life-giving Spirit, which empowers us to live in hope (8 : 1-17). Indeed, we Christians live in an absolutely certain and assured hope for a God-given future which will exceedingly surpass our present sufferings (8 : 18-39).

A. We Christians "Boast" of a Hope Which Never Puts Us to Shame: Rom 5 : 1-11

As Paul proclaims, now that "we Christians have been justified by faith, we enjoy a wonderfully new relationship of "peace" with God through our Lord Jesus Christ (5 : 1). That God has graciously established a new situation of peace[1] with us means we are no longer God's "enemies" but have been "reconciled" with him (5 : 10-11). This new peace and reconciliation from God thus rectifies the dire hopelessness of our being weak, ungodly sinners destined for the horrible "wrath" of God (5 : 6-9; 1 : 18 – 3 : 20).[2] And

---

[1] This situation of "peace with God" in 5 : 1 does not refer to a subjective or psychological state acquired by the believer, a feeling of "peace of mind," but rather to an objective relationship that God has freely given and established between himself and those he has justified by faith. See Schlier, *Römerbrief,* 141; M. Wolter, *Rechtfertigung und zukünftiges Heil. Untersuchungen zu Röm 5,1-11* (BZNW 43; Berlin/New York: de Gruyter, 1978) 95; W. Foerster, "*eirēnē,*" *TDNT* 2 (1964) 415-416.

[2] Wolter (*Rechtfertigung,* 103-104) points out how "peace" in 5 : 1 b stands in opposition and contrast to the "wrath of God" in 1 : 18.

so we are now standing within a new and hopeful dimension of God's "grace" to which we have now gained access in faith through our exalted Lord Jesus Christ (5 : 2 a).

In addition to placing us in a new and *present* situation of God's grace, peace and reconciliation, our having been justified by faith stimulates us to a new and joyful hope of participating in the *future* glory of God. And so, "we boast of hope for the glory of God" (5 : 2 b). Both "boasting" (*kauchaomai*) and "hope" (*elpis*) express the idea of confidence, trust or reliance; "hope" is an act or attitude of confidence in the future completion of God's salvific activity, whereas "boasting" is a deep, delightful and joyous reliance upon something worthy to form the foundation of one's life in relation to God and his fellow human beings.[3] By this exaggerated expression Paul places great stress and accentuation upon the attitude of Christian hope—he boldly proclaims the completely joyful confidence he and his fellow Christians have of their hope for God's future completion of his salvific activity. It is a heightened overstatement of hope—not only do "we" Christians possess a present hope for the future, but we even go so far as to "boast" of this hope, to rejoice, take delight in and be deeply confident of it. Our "boasting of hope" thus supersedes the Jewish empty "boasting" of the works of the Law as a foundation for one's life before God (2 : 17.23; 3 : 27; 4 : 2). We Christians have genuine grounds for a truly reliable "boasting," as we "boast" of our hope for the future glory of God!

The "glory of God" (*doxēs tou theou*) serves as a comprehensive term for the manifestation of God's divine mode of being, his radiance, splendor or power, in and through his salvific and creative activity.[4] Here it designates the future completion of God's salvific and creative activity which he has already begun to display in the revelation of the definitive "righteousness of God" (1 : 16-17; 3 : 21-26). This new and decisive justification by God eradicates the horrible hopelessness of all of us who have sinned so that we lack the "glory of God" (3 : 23). Justified, reconciled and forgiven by God, then, we Christians can boldly and jubilantly "boast" of our hope of participating in the future, final "glory of God" (5 : 2 b).[5]

We Christians "boast" not only of our great hope for the future, but, quite astonishingly and paradoxically, we even "boast" of our present "suf-

---

[3] Schlier, *Römerbrief,* 143.

[4] O. Kuss (*Der Römerbrief* (Erste Lieferung (Röm 1,1 bis 6,11); 2 d ed.; Regensburg: Pustet, 1963) 615) states that the "glory of God" is not only a salvific benefit but the summation of all salvific benefits.

[5] Paul further develops our hope for the "glory of God" in Rom 8 : 17-39. For other uses and occurrences of the "glory (*doxa*) of God" in Romans, see 1 : 23; 3 : 7; 6 : 4; 8 : 18.21; 9 : 4.23; 15 : 7. "Glory" is also used in the sense of praising or "giving glory" to God, see 4 : 20; 11 : 36; 16 : 27.

ferings" (5 : 3 a). "Suffering" (*thlipsis*) includes not only the painful tribulations and oppression that Christians may undergo externally or internally for the sake of their faith, but also the general afflictions, distress and anxiety one normally encounters in life.[6] How can painful "sufferings," then, induce the joyous self-glorying and delight connoted by "boasting"? And what is even more puzzling, how can "sufferings" form the foundation for one's life before God and be the grounds for the "boasting" of complete confidence in God's future?

This perplexing paradox is explained by the actual, lived experience of Christian hope as described through a rhetorical "gradatio," a chain-like series of expressions building to a dramatic climax (5 : 3-4).[7] When we Christians who have hope (5 : 2 b) encounter sufferings we experience that suffering produces for us an attitude of "steadfastness" (5 : 3 b).[8] Paul often associates such steadfastness" (*hypomonē*) with "hope" (*elpis*) in contexts of suffering.[9] "Steadfastness" thus refers to an attitude of patient perseverance or *endurance* which actively withstands continual opposition or distress (see Rom 8 : 25; 12 : 12; 15 : 4-5). For us Christians who have hope, then, our suffering causes not a loss or destruction of hope but a transformation from hope to patient steadfastness. In other words, our suffering effectively brings about the steadfast, enduring or persevering aspect of our attitude of hope.

Our steadfastness, in turn, produces "provedness" (*dokimēn*, 5 : 4 a), "proven character" or "the quality of being approved."[10] It designates a

---

[6] BAGD, 362; H. Schlier, "*thlibō*," *TDNT* 3 (1965) 143-148; *Römerbrief*, 146. "Suffering" introduces another theme to be treated more fully in Rom 8 : 17-39.

[7] A rhetorical "gradatio" is a continuing repetition in which the last member of a syntactical group is repeated as the first member of the following group. This chain-like repetition emphatically raises the expression from one level to the next, and often, as here, further explains the expression. The "gradatio" in 5 : 3-4 exemplifies the "modus per incrementa" in which the strongest member of the series, in this case *elpida*, "hope" (5 : 4 b), is placed in the final emphatic position. See Lausberg, *Rhetorik*, § 619, 623, 653, 451.

[8] It should be kept in mind, however, that the "experience" described in the "gradatio" in 5 : 3-4 is not a subjective or psychological process, as if illustrating the way that suffering can psychologically be the cause of hope. Rather, the attitude of hope is presupposed from 5 : 2 b, so that what is being described is an objective experience common to Christians within or as a result of their attitude of hope. See Schlier, *Römerbrief*, 148.

[9] F. Hauck, "*hypomenō*," *TDNT* 4 (1967) 583; BAGD, 845-846. There are several passages elsewhere in Paul where *hypomonē* is closely associated with the attitude of hope and/or refers to steadfastness in the midst of opposition and suffering: 1 Cor 13 : 7; 2 Cor 1 : 6-7; 6 : 4; 12 : 12; 1 Thes 1 : 3.

[10] BAGD, 202; Zerwick and Grosvenor, *Analysis*, 469; Cranfield, *Romans*, 261. See also W. Grundmann, "*dokimos*," *TDNT* 2 (1964) 255-260.

state of having been tested, of having withstood trials or tribulations. Hence, we Christians who have endured sufferings with steadfastness experience that we have been tested and approved.

Finally and climactically, our provedness produces "hope" (*elpida*, 5:4b). We Christians who have been tested and approved by steadfast suffering thus experience a renewal of hope. Rather than eliminating hope, suffering ultimately revives and nourishes our hope. And so, this is why we Christians can boldly "boast" even of our sufferings—they actually stimulate, renew and increase the hope of which we "boast" (5:2b). Similar to the hope of Abraham (4:18-21), our attitude of Christian hope remains entirely realistic. It takes into account and embraces any and all possible suffering one might meet throughout life. That the inevitable sufferings of human living instigate and incite us to hope all the more (5:3b-4) assures the reliability, growth and strength of our Christian hope. This vibrant hope, then, never stagnates but subsists as a dynamic phenomenon always open to a new and greater growth.

Furthermore, this dynamic "hope" (*elpis*) of ours "does not shame" us (5:5a), that is, it does not place us in a situation of objective "shame" before God. On the contrary, God himself upholds and guarantees our hope. For God has abundantly "poured out"[11] his love into our inmost being, "our hearts,"[12] through his Holy Spirit, "given" to us Christians (5:5b) now standing under the divine power of "grace" (5:2a).[13] God demonstrated his "love" in that while we were still mired in the hopelessness of being weak (5:6a), ungodly (5:6b), sinners (5:8) Christ died on our behalf. God's love "toward us" in Christ's death "for us" (5:8) far exceeds even the possible but rare heroism in which someone might dare to die for the sake of a just or good person. God demonstrates *his own*[14] unique love toward us by the humanly inconceivable fact that Christ died for our sake precisely when we were still "sinners" (5:8), that is, when we were not "just" or "good" (5:7), and when we were not yet "justified" (5:1a.9a), but languishing in

---

[11] "Has been poured out" (*ekkechytai*) is often used in the OT to express the divinely abundant outpouring of God's gifts. See BAGD, 247; Schlier, *Römerbrief,* 150.

[12] "Heart" (*kardia*) refers to the inner life of a person, to the "core" of one's being; it is "the source or seat of all the forces and functions of soul and spirit." See J. Behm, "*kardia,*" *TDNT* 3 (1965) 611.

[13] For the close connection between "grace" (*charis*) and the idea of "gift" or "giving," see I. de la Potterie, "*Charis* paulinienne et *charis* johannique," *Jesus und Paulus* (Festschrift für W. G. Kümmel zum 70. Geburtstag; ed. E. E. Ellis and E. Gräßer; Göttingen: Vandenhoeck & Ruprecht, 1975) 268.

[14] Cranfield, *Romans,* 265: "*heautou* is emphatic, God's love being contrasted with that shown by men (v. 7)."

miserable hopelessness. Thus, the love which God continues to "demonstrate" (*synistēsin*, 5 : 8)[15] is the love he still "pours out" into our hearts (5 : 5 b), so that the "hope for the glory of God" of which we now gladly "boast" (5 : 2 b) "does not shame" (5 : 5 a) or disappoint us.

Paul continues to illustrate the secure sureness of our Christian hope for the future with exuberant exclamations of its utter certainty. Now that we have been justified by the expiatory death ("blood") of Christ, "how much more then,"[16] that is, how certainly, can we have the sure hope that "we *will* be saved" from God's wrath through Christ (5 : 9). Correlatively, now that we who were obstinate "enemies"[17] of God have been "reconciled"[18] to God through the death of his Son, "how much more," how surely, do we exclaim the secure hope that "we *will* be saved" by his life (5 : 10). Our justification and reconciliation by God arouses the absolutely assured hope that we *will be saved* from the terrible hopelessness of God's wrath as we share in the new "life" of the risen Lord Jesus Christ. And not only do we boldly "boast" of our hope for God's future glory (5 : 2 b) and "boast" even of our present sufferings (5 : 3), but, "now" that we have received reconciliation through our Lord Jesus Christ, Paul climactically concludes that we are all the while joyfully and confidently "boasting" in *God himself* (5 : 11), the ultimate foundation and goal of our hope.

As we have seen, Paul began achieving his purpose of stimulating the hope of the Romans, that they be "strengthened" and "mutually encouraged" (1 : 11-12), with his own strong and encouraging display of the hope of "not being ashamed of the gospel" (1 : 16 a). The sure "hope" of which we Christians boldly "boast" (5 : 2 b) and which "does not shame" us (5 : 5 a) corre-

---

[15] On the present tense here Cranfield (*Romans,* 265) states: "The use of the present tense is noteworthy: the event of the Cross is a past event (*apethanen*), but the fact that it occurred remains as a present proof."

[16] "How much more then" (*pollō oun mallon*) exemplifies the *qal wāḥômer* conclusion, the first exegetical rule of Rabbi Hillel; see Strack, *Einleitung,* 97; StrB, 3. 223-226; Michel, *Römer,* 182 n. 28; C. Mauerer, "Der Schluß "a minore ad majus" als Element paulinischer Theologie," *TLZ* 85 (1960) 149-152; H. Müller, Der rabbinische Qal-Wachomer-Schluß in paulinischer Typologie," *ZNW* 58 (1967) 73-92.

[17] "Enemies" (*echthroi*) in 5 : 10 a has an active sense of rebellion or disobedience against God, like the related "enmity" or "hostility" (*echthra*) in 8 : 7; see W. Foerster, "*echthros,*" *TDNT* 2 (1964) 814-815.

[18] On the concept of "reconciliation" in Paul, F. Büchsel, "*allassō,*" *TDNT* 1 (1964) 255-258; O. Hofius, "Erwägungen zur Gestalt und Herkunft des paulinischen Versöhnungsgedankens," *ZTK* 77 (1980) 186-199; "'Gott hat unter uns aufgerichtet das Wort der Versöhnung' (2 Kor 5.19)," *ZNW* 71 (1980) 3-20; R. P. Martin, *Reconciliation. A Study of Paul's Theology* (New Foundations Theological Library; Atlanta: Knox, 1981) 140-154; J. A. Fitzmyer, "Reconciliation in Pauline Theology," *To Advance the Gospel,* 162-185.

sponds to Paul's own confident pronouncement of lively hope. Paul's not
being ashamed of the gospel voices a hope in the "power of God" to bring
all who believe to future, final "salvation" (*eis sōtērian*, 1 : 16 b). And likewise the hope of which we Christians boast does not shame because it is a
hope in the "love of God" (5 : 5 b.8) to bring those who are justified and
reconciled by faith (5 : 1.9-10) to final eschatological salvation (*sōthēsometha*,
5 : 9.10). In both instances hope is directed toward the future completion of
God's salvific activity and is expressed as an attitude of "not being shamed"
because it is presently being upheld by God himself. And so we see that
Paul continues to stir up a strong and encouraging hope in his fellow Christians at Rome, as he forcefully and forthrightly proclaims not only his own
confident hope (1 : 16-17) but the secure and sure hope that all Christians
share with him (5 : 1-11).

We have also observed how Paul stressed the "in hope" aspect of Abraham's faith (4 : 18-21) and strongly implied (4 : 23-25) that since hope was an
essential characteristic of Abraham's justification by faith (4 : 22), hope is
likewise an essential consequence of the justification of Christians who share
the faith of Abraham their father (4 : 12.16). Striking similarities are evident
between the hope of Abraham and that of Christians : First, the hope of both
is totally realistic, taking full account of the weakness or sufferings of the
human condition, which seems to obstruct God's salvific action and contradict hope. Abraham's hope, rather than being weakened or destroyed in
view of his human situation (4 : 19), was actually "strengthened" (4 : 20) to a
"full conviction" (4 : 21). And rather than destroying Christian hope, suffering increases and strengthens it (5 : 3-4), so that we Christians can even
"boast" of our sufferings (5 : 3 a). In the hope of both a consideration of the
human reality which seems to contradict hope in fact instigates and incites an
even stronger hope. Second, the joyful praise and total confidence in God
connoted by "boasting" as an expression of Christian hope (5 : 2-3.11) corresponds to Abraham's "giving glory to God" (4 : 20 b) and being "fully convinced" (4 : 21) as an expression of his hope. Both Abraham and we Christians manifest hope as an attitude of present joy, praising God now, while
being confidently convinced of participating in the future completion of
God's salvific activity. [19]

---

[19] Paul avoids using "boasting" for Abraham's hope (see 4 : 2) but does employ it
for Christian hope. There is, of course, a basic difference between the hope of Abraham and that of Christians, which is based upon what God has done for us in the
Christ event. But Paul concentrates upon the similarity between the faith and hope of
Christians and the hopeful faith of Abraham, "our father."

B. Our Christian Hope Greatly Surpasses Hopelessness: Rom 5:12-21.

Having vigorously proclaimed the reliable, vibrantly realistic hope that comes from our being justified by faith (5:1-11), Paul compares and contrasts this new situation of hope with that of hopelessness (5:12-21). The grim hopelessness that engulfs all of humanity originated through "one man," Adam, the "first" human being, who representatively embodies all mankind. Through his primal sin the contagious power of sin entered the world and through sin the power of death, which destroys life and thus extinguishes all hope for the future,[20] spread to all human beings, inasmuch as all indeed have sinned (5:12; see also 3:9.23). The death-bringing power of sin poisoned the world even before the Law was given (5:13), for death "reigned" from Adam to Moses (the Law) even over those who did not sin by transgressing a direct command of God like Adam did (5:13-14). But this "first" Adam, the instigator for the hope-negating powers of sin and death, is a "type" (typos) who points to a "second," eschatological Adam "who was to come" (5:14), the originator and mediator of a new hope for all.

Although through the trespass of the "one" (Adam) the "many" (polloi = all)[21] died bereft of any hope for future life, the grace of God freely given through the "one" man Jesus Christ overwhelmingly "abounded" (eperisseusen) to the "many" (all) (5:15). This gracious gift was occasioned by "many" trespasses and thus offsets and more than compensates for the judgment which proceeded from "one" (Adam); and this gracious gift leads ultimately to God's future, final "justification," which thus eliminates the hopelessness of future, final "condemnation" (5:16). Through the trespass of the "one" the hope defeating power of death established its oppressive reign of hopelessness through the "one" Adam (5:17 a). But those who now receive the overwhelming "abundance" (perisseian) of the gracious gift of righteousness have a supremely certain hope that they "will reign" in future, final "life" through the "one" Jesus Christ (5:17), the originator and mediator of a new hope. This eminently sure hope for future "life" established through Jesus Christ thus eradicates and abundantly supersedes the despair-bringing power of "death" established through Adam.

Just as surely as God's future "condemnation" comes through the trespass of the "one" Adam and extends to all humans, so also God's "justification" which is tantamount to future "life"[22] now comes through the righ-

---

[20] R. Bultmann, "thanatos," TDNT 3 (1965) 14-21; Schlier, Römerbrief, 160-161.

[21] Jeremias, "polloi," 164-166.

[22] An epexegetical genitive or genitive of direction and goal; see Schlier, Römerbrief, 174; Wilckens, Römer, 1.326 n. 1095.

teous deed of the "one" Jesus Christ and likewise extends to all (5 : 18). For just as surely as it was through the "disobedience" of Adam that all (the "many") "were constituted" (*katestathēsan*) hopeless sinners, so now it is through the "obedience" of Jesus Christ that all may now grasp the firm and solid hope that they "*will* be constituted" (*katastathēsontai*) righteous (5 : 19). [23]

The Law actually contributes to hopelessness as it intensifies the deadly power of sin by assigning it a decisive eschatological quality and definitive universality (see Rom 7 : 7-24). For the Law came in after sin (see 5 : 12-14) so that the trespass might increase all the more (5 : 20 a). But precisely where the hopeless power of sin increased, the hopeful power of God's grace "superabounded" (5 : 20 b) and has thus more than overcome the power of sin for despair. And so, just as certainly as sin "reigned" and dominated through the despair that is death, so now grace may "reign" and predominate over despair because of the righteousness which induces the hope for future, "eternal life" through our Lord Jesus Christ (5 : 21), the mediator of this new hope.

Precisely in the midst of the pervasive powers of sin and death, then, we may manifest a definitively certain hope for God's future eternal life, a hope that eradicates, totally overpowers and abundantly exceeds the dreadful hopelessness effected by sin and death. But exactly how can this hope for a *future* life predominate over the *present* hopelessness we still experience through sin and death?

C. We Christians Can Already Live the New Life for Which We Hope: Rom 6 : 1-14

With diatribal musings Paul clarifies how our new hope can predominate over hopelessness. He queries whether we are to continue in sin so that grace may increase (6 : 1). In other words, is the life for which we may now hope exclusively for the future, so that we must remain locked within the hopelessness of still sinning now? Indeed, should we not purposely continue to sin precisely in order to induce an ever greater increase of grace (5 : 20 b), and hence an even greater hope (5 : 21 b)? "By no means!" is Paul's resounding reply. That would transform our sincere and humble hope into a perverted presumption upon God's freely given grace, as it would ultimately

---

[23] The future tenses in both 5 : 17 b (will reign) and 5 : 19 b (will be made) we take as eschatological futures; see Schlier, *Römerbrief,* 172, 175; Michel, *Römer,* 191. These future tense verbs exemplify expressions of hope which do not employ an explicit word for "hope". See Chapter I.

make human sin rather than God's grace the stimulus for our hope. No, as those who have "died to sin," how can we still "live" in it (6 : 2)? Our hope is not, then, merely a matter of future life, but of "living" now.

As Paul explains, it is because we have already "died" to the power of sin that we may "live" already the "life" for which we hope. All of us who were baptized into Christ Jesus were baptized into his "death" (6 : 3). We were therefore "buried"[24] with him through baptism into "death," so that as Christ was raised from the dead through the glory of the Father, so now we might "walk," that is, "live"[25] in "newness of life" (6 : 4). This "newness of life" is the same new, future and final "life" (5 : 17 b.18 b.21 b) for which we hope. Our future hope, then, can already begin to exist for us as a present, "living" reality. The assured hope we have of sharing in the future, resurrected life of Christ inspires us to start "living" out our future hope by already "walking" in the "newness of life." For if we have been and still are united with the likeness of Christ's death, then we have the sure hope that "we *will*" also share in his resurrection (6 : 5).

That we can already live the new life for which we hope means we need not remain enslaved in morbid hopelessness by living under the power of sin. Our "old" self has been crucified with Christ through baptism. Thus our "body of sin," our old sinful self, has been destroyed, so that we need no longer be hopelessly enslaved to the power of sin (6 : 6). For one who has already died (with Christ in baptism) has been and still is effectively liberated from the deadly power of sin (6 : 7).

If we have already died with Christ in baptism, then, we "believe," that is, we have the certain hope[26] that we also "*will live with*" him (6 : 8). We know that Christ, being raised from the dead, can die no more; the hopelessness that is "death" no longer holds power over him (6 : 9). The death he died he "died to sin once for all" (6 : 10 a). Since, then, Christ obediently submitted himself to the full consequence of the power of sin, namely, "death," the power of sin has been "once for all," unrepeatably and definitively, exhausted upon him, so that death can no longer exert any power over him. Death can never again deprive him of life. For the life he now lives, he "lives to God" (6 : 10 b). He died in submission to the deadly power of sin, but he now "lives" in submission and service to God. And this inspires us to make the future hope that "we will live with him" (6 : 8 b) an already present and "living" reality. For we must now consider ourselves "dead" indeed to the hopelessness that is sin, but "living" to the hopefulness of humbly submitting to and serving God in and with Christ Jesus (6 : 11).

---

[24] Burial here signifies the completion and confirmation of death; see Schlier, *Römerbrief,* 193.

[25] BAGD, 649; Zerwick and Grosvenor, *Analysis,* 471; Schlier, *Römerbrief,* 194.

[26] As oriented to the future, "we believe" here actually expresses hope.

Paul draws out the moral consequences of the hope we live by now being "dead to sin but living to God" (6:11): We are not to allow the deadly power of sin to continue to reign in our still mortal bodies by obeying its evil desires (6:12). We are no longer to yield the members of our bodies to the menacing power of sin as weapons of wrongdoing (6:13 a). Rather, we should yield ourselves to God as those who have been rescued from the gruesome hopelessness of being as good as "dead" to the hope of "living" (6:13 b). And yield the members of our bodies to the service of God as weapons of righteousness (6:13 c). We are now able to live out our hope by living out all of these imperatives because of our confidently certain hope that the power of sin "*will not dominate*" over us, for we are not under the Law but under the grace of God (6:14).

Hence, it is *possible* for us Christians to live already, as part of our "living" hope, the new future life for which we hope. But not only is it *possible*, it is even *necessary* for us to live this new life of hope now.

D. We Christians Must Live the New Life of Hope: Rom 6:15-23

Paul raises another diatribal musing: Does the firm hope that "sin *will not dominate*" (6:14 a) over us, mean, then, that we are free to sin now, that "we *may* sin," within our new realm of hope founded on not being "under the Law but under grace" (6:15)? In other words, although it is now possible for us to escape the poisonous power of sin (6:1-14), are we nevertheless permitted to commit sins within or because of our new hope? "By no means!" Paul thunders. Sin and our new life of hope are completely incompatible and diametrically opposed, for if we return to acts of sin, we inevitably return to our former hopelessness. With vivid "slavery/freedom" imagery Paul explains why Christians who live in hope not only *can* but *must* not sin. Both hope and hopelessness are constituted by a fiercely "slavish obedience" with contradictory results. As Paul tells us, when you offer yourselves in "slavish obedience" to anyone, you are "slaves" of the one you "obey" (6:16 a). If we return to sinning, we remain obedient slaves to sin and have returned to the hopelessness in which our inescapable destiny is future, final "death". But in our new life of hope we are "slaves" to the "obedience" of faith (see 1:5; 10:16) in which our inevitable destiny is future, final "righteousness" (6:16 b).

Paul thanks God that although his Christian audience were once hopeless "slaves" of sin, they have now begun to be obedient in faith from the heart to the form of teaching to which they were committed (6:17). But although they as Christians have been freed *from* sin (6:18 a), this does not mean that they are now "free" *to* sin, for there is a sense in which they have once again become "slaves". Indeed, in weak, human terms which cannot adequately capture the divine reality involved here (6 : 19 a), they have again been "enslaved," not to the horrid hopelessness of sin with a future destiny of death (6 : 16 b) but to God's "righteousness," the future goal of hope (6 : 18 b.16 b). Our hope for the eschatological righteousness of God, then, can and must be lived out now (see 1 : 17 b) as a "slavery to righteousness". For just as we once slavishly submitted ourselves to immorality and to iniquity which in turn led to further iniquity, so now we *must* submit ourselves as "slaves" to righteousness which leads to "holiness," our sanctification by God (6 : 19 b).

It is true that when we were "slaves" to the power of sin, we then could have considered ourselves "free" with regard to righteousness (6 : 20). But in that situation we were bereft of any real hope for the future. For what "fruit" or future hope could we then expect from the sinful things of which we are now ashamed before God,[27] since the future goal of those things is the hopeless finality of "death" (6 : 21)? But now, freed from sin while at the same time "enslaved" to God, we have a true, authentic hope for God's future, since the "fruit" of our living out hope now as "enslaved" to God is "holiness" from God, whose future goal is eternal life (6 : 22). Therefore, as Christians we *can* and *must* not sin now (6 : 15), for the only "wages," the inevitable end product, that sin rewards is "death" (6 : 23 a). But our already present future hope that is firmly founded on God's "free gift" is "eternal life" in Christ Jesus our Lord (6 : 23 b). And now that we stand under the power of God's grace (6 : 15), we *can* and *must* live even now this future, eternal life for which we hope.

But now that we are "under grace," we are no longer "under the Law" (6 : 15), and this carries consequences for our hope.

E. We Christians Are Now Freed from the Hopelessness of the Law for the Hope of the Spirit: Rom 7 : 1-6

The Law can no longer exert its powerful influence over us because the Law can rule over someone only as long as that person is living (7 : 1). For example, a married woman is bound by law to her husband as long as he lives; but if her husband dies she is released from the law concerning the

---

[27] In 1 : 16 Paul's "not being ashamed" is an expression of hope based on the gospel and oriented to God's future salvation; in 6 : 21 "you are ashamed" is related to the Christian's present hope, which includes a recognition of past sinfulness oriented to future death. See also 5 : 5 a: "hope does not shame..."

husband (7 : 2). While her husband still lives she will be called an adulteress
if she gives herself to another man. But if her husband dies she is free from
the law, so that she is not an adulteress if she marries another (7 : 3). Similarly, we Christians have in effect died to the "lordship" of the Law through
the body of Christ, so that we now belong to another "lord," namely, the
one who has been raised from the dead. Our sacramental union with the
death and resurrection of Christ through our baptism (6 : 3-5), then, gives us
the hope that we can and must "produce fruit for God" (7 : 4),[28] the "fruit"
which brings us future, "eternal life" (6 : 22).

That we may now produce fruit for God means we can and must no
longer live entrenched in the ominous hopelessness we had while under the
power of the Law. For when we were "in the flesh" (our situation before
our baptism), the Law activated the sinful passions within us "to produce
fruit for death" (7 : 5). While under the sway of the Law, we were hopelessly
destined for future, final "death," the "fruit" of our life of sin (6 : 21). But
now that we have been cut loose from the grip of the Law, "dead" to that
menace in which we were desperately entangled, we can and must freely live
out our new hope for God's future by serving God now in the "newness of
the Spirit" rather than in what has now become the "oldness of the letter" of
the Law (7 : 6).

Paul goes on to further express and explain our extreme despair under
the oldness of the letter of the Law (7 : 7-25) as the backdrop for his spirited
proclamation of the robust hope that is now ours as we serve God in the
newness of the Spirit (8 : 1-17).

F. The Law of Sin and Death Brings us Despair: Rom 7 : 7-25

If it was through the Law that sinful passions operated within us so that
our hopeless destiny was death (7 : 5), Paul queries whether the Law, then,
can actually be considered "sin" (7 : 7 a)? "By no means!" he retorts. But
it is true that "I," which refers not just to Paul but to "us" and every person
before being baptized,[29] would not have experienced the malignant power of
sin had it not been for the Law (7 : 7 b). For "I" would not have known the
sinfulness of "coveting" if the Law had not said, "You shall not covet"
(Exod 20 : 17; Deut 5 : 21) (7 : 7 c). But the penetrating power of sin slyly

---

[28] The purpose clause in 7 : 4 is at the same time an indirect imperative. Hence,
"we *can and must* produce fruit for God." See Schlier, *Römerbrief*, 217.

[29] Wilckens, *Römer*, 2. 76-78; Schlier, *Römerbrief*, 221.

took its opportunity through the commandment of the Law and awakened in "me" all manner of coveting (7 : 8 a). For without the Law sin is "dead," that is, dormant and without its full force (7 : 8 b). At one time "I" was living without the Law, but when the commandment of the Law arrived the power of sin "came to life" (7 : 9) and "I" in effect "died" (7 : 10 a).[30] Thus, the very commandment which was intended to lead to "life" actually inflicted me with the hopeless destiny of "death" (7 : 10 b; see Gen 2 : 16-17). Since the Law wanted to prevent "me" from falling into the clutches of sin and thus incurring future "death," it originally inspired hope for "life". But in the Law's very prohibition not to sin the power to sin became fully activated and thus deceived "me" by misusing the Law and transforming it from a foundation for hope into a weapon for the despair of "death" (7 : 11). Nevertheless, the Law itself remains holy, and the commandment holy, just and good (7 : 12).

But if the "good" Law ultimately destines "me" for death, are we not forced to admit that what is in itself "good" (the Law) has actually become for "me" the cause for the despair that is "death"? "By no means!" Paul vehemently insists. For it was sin, in order that it might prove itself to be sin, that destined me for death through the good Law, so that sin might become sinful to the extreme through the commandment (7 : 13). The "spiritual" Law, then, simply lacks the power necessary to effect within the "fleshly" me the hope for life it was meant to stimulate. Although the Law commanded me not to sin (7 : 7 d), it cannot prevent me from being totally "sold under" and enslaved to the deadly power of sin. I am so much in bondage to the power of sin that I do not even realize what I am bringing about; for I do not do what I want, but what I hate (7 : 15). If I do what I do not want, I thereby agree with the Law that it is "good" (7 : 16), as the Law tries to prevent me from doing what I hate. Hence, I am able to agree with the Law, but, shackled by the power of sin, I am not able to do the good that the Law commands.

So overwhelmed by the deceitful power of sin am I that it is not even "I" who does what I hate but the power of sin dwelling within me (7 : 17). Thus, the power of sin extends to the very interior, the core, of the human person, so that the mere will to do the good advised by the Law is not enough to overcome the indwelling power of sin as the cause of hopelessness (7 : 18-20). The Law, then, cannot rescue "me" from this dilemma of despair brought on by this "extreme sinfulness" (7 : 13 d) of the power of sin. Wanting to accomplish the good, "I" discover and experience the "Law"[31]

---

[30] In all probability an allusion to the situation of Adam, mankind, in Gen 2-3. See Wilckens, *Römer*, 2. 78-82; Schlier, *Römerbrief*, 224; S. Lyonnet, "L'histoire du salut selon le chapitre VII de l'épître aux Romains," *Bib* 43 (1962) 117-151.

[31] A figurative use of *nomos* in the sense of "rule" or "regularity" ("Gesetzmäßig-

that evil clings to me (7 : 21). I readily agree with the Law of God according to my inner self, but I perceive another "Law"[32] within my body at war with the "Law" of my mind (the Law of God with which I agree; 7 : 16.22) and making me captive (see 7 : 6) to the "Law" of sin[33] within my body (7 : 22-23).

Here we have reached the highpoint of our dilemma of despair with regard to the Law: The good and spiritual Law of God, which tried to induce hope for life by prohibiting sin, and with which "I" could interiorly agree, is the very same Law that the power of sin dwelling within my interior has deceptively transformed into the "Law" of sin for me. That is why the commandment of the Law which intended to incite hope for life became the absolute hopelessness of death for "me" (7 : 10). Accordingly, the depth of this despair comes to its climactic, lamentful expression: "O wretched person that I am! Who will rescue me from this body of death?" (7 : 24).[34]

Paul immediately blurts out a preliminary response to this desperate plea for deliverance from the despair of death with a thanksgiving—"thanks be to God through Jesus Christ our Lord!" (7 : 25 a). But before proclaiming the saving hope that is ours in answer to the lament of hopelessness (7 : 24), Paul succinctly sums up this absolute dilemma of despair in which "I" was totally enslaved before being freed by Christ in baptism: "So then, as one and the same "I," "I" serve the Law of God with my mind (7 : 16 b.22.23), while with my flesh I serve the Law of sin (7 : 25 b; see 7 : 21-23).[35]

---

keit," in Schlier, *Römerbrief,* 234), but still in reference to the Mosaic Law; see Wilkens, *Römer,* 2. 89; H. Räisänen, Das 'Gesetz des Glaubens' (Röm. 3.27) und das 'Gesetz des Geistes' (Röm. 8.2)," *NTS* 26 (1979-80) 101-117, esp. 113.

[32] Another figurative use of *nomos* in the sense of an active force or power, but still with reference to the Mosaic Law. See Schlier, *Römerbrief,* 234; Wilckens, *Römer,* 2. 89.

[33] The Mosaic Law as misused and dominated by the power of sin; see Schlier, *Römerbrief,* 234; Wilckens, *Römer,* 2. 89-94.

[34] The conflict between "wanting" and "doing" as described in 7 : 14-24 is not a subjective, psychological process but an objective, real dilemma of utter despair; see Schlier, *Römerbrief,* 230-232.

[35] Despite the alleged problem of this final repetition of despair in 7 : 25 b immediately after the thanksgiving of 7 : 25 a, we find no convincing reason to regard it as a gloss, since it can be satisfactorily interpreted in relation to 7 : 14-23. As Cranfield (*Romans,* 368) says: "... an exegesis which rests on a re-arrangement of sentences or on the exclusion of an alleged gloss, when there is not the slightest suggestion of support in the textual tradition for either procedure, is exceedingly hazardous, and, when sense can be made of the text as it stands, has little claim to be regarded as responsible."

G. The Law of the Spirit of Life Brings Us Hope: Rom 8 : 1-17

In answer to our woeful plea for rescue from the despair of being destined for the future finality of "death" (7 : 24), Paul zestfully announces the confident hope that there will be no future, final "condemnation" to death for those now in union with Christ Jesus through baptism (8 : 1). For the Law of the Spirit of life in Christ Jesus has wondrously liberated us (the imprisoned "I" in 7 : 23) from the Law of sin and death (8 : 2). This new "Law" of the Spirit of life refers to the rule and directives for how we are now to live[36] determined and dominated by the power of God's Spirit rather than the power of sin (see 7 : 14-23). This "Law" of God's Spirit thus stimulates us to hope for future, final "life" in Christ Jesus, since it has freed us from the "Law" of sin, God's directives for life as dominated and transformed by the power of sin, and thus from the despair of future, final "death".

God himself graciously rectified the inability of his good and spiritual Law to be the hope for life it was meant to be (7 : 10), after it had been weakened through the flesh. He sent his own Son in the "likeness"[37] of sinful flesh for the removal or atonement of sin and thus condemned sin in the flesh (8 : 3). Hence, we may now have the sure hope of no "condemnation" to death (8 : 1), because God has already "condemned" sin, the root cause of our condemnation to death (5 : 16.18; 7 : 23-24), precisely where the power of sin was operative—"in the flesh". God thus condemned sin and eliminated its power to effect "death" through the death to sin of his Son (6 : 9-10) sent in the likeness of the very same flesh the power of sin had dominated.

Since God has eradicated sin's deceitful power over us, we may now fulfill the just requirement of the Law and live not according to our sinful flesh but according to God's Spirit (8 : 4). This means we can now live with an authentic hope for God's future. For those determined by the flesh "aspire" (phronousin)[38] for the concerns of the flesh (8 : 5 a), which lead ultimately to "death" (8 : 6 a). But we who are determined by the Spirit aspire for the

---

[36] Hence, a figurative use of *nomos* but in reference to the Torah as God's instructions and directives for living. See Schlier, *Römerbrief,* 238-239; Wilckens, *Römer,* 2. 122-123.

[37] Wilckens, *Römer,* 2. 125-126. This "likeness" includes an identity in non-identity; it is not an identity insofar as Christ was God's own (sinless) Son, but more than a mere resemblance insofar as Christ was truly of human "flesh". See Zerwick and Grosvenor, *Analysis,* 475; BAGD, 567.

[38] BAGD, 866; G. Bertram, "*phrēn,*" *TDNT* 9 (1974) 232-233.

concerns of the Spirit (8 : 5 b), which lead ultimately to "life and peace" (8 : 6 b) with God. The aspiration of the flesh leads not to peace with God but to enmity against God, since it is unable to obey the Law of God (8 : 7). Those still living in accord with the flesh then cannot please God (8 : 8), and thus find themselves powerless to live out God's directives for life in order to have a firm foundation for hope in God.

But we Christians are now empowered to live out a vigorous hope enlivened by the Spirit of God which now dwells within us (8 : 9). If Christ's Spirit resides within us, then, although our body is virtually "dead" because of sin, the Spirit brings us "life" because of righteousness (8 : 10). Indeed, if the Spirit of him who raised Jesus from the dead dwells within us, then we may surely and confidently hope that he who raised Christ from the dead "*will give life*" also to our still mortal bodies through this indwelling Spirit (8 : 11). And this hope for life based on the power of the Spirit dwelling within us (8 : 9-11) through our baptism is precisely what we needed to effectively overcome the despair of death based on the power of sin dwelling within our earthly, human bodies of "flesh" (7 : 17.20.23).

Thus, it is absolutely imperative that we no longer live according to the flesh, otherwise we cannot possibly escape the doom of despair as we are surely destined to die (8 : 12-13 a). We can and must live according to God's Spirit, then, for if by God's Spirit we "put to death" the sinful deeds of our body of sin, we have the secure hope that we "*will live*" (8 : 13 b) a future, final life with God.

Our present status as "sons of God" (8 : 14) assures the certainty of our hope for God's future. When baptized we did not receive a spirit of slavery returning us to the terrible fear of eschatological death we had while hopelessly enslaved to the Law of sin and death (see 7 : 24; 8 : 2). No, we were endowed with the Spirit of sonship, in which we may confidently cry, "Abba! Father!" (8 : 15). This Spirit thus assures us interiorly that since we are already "sons," "children," and "heirs," we hold a firm and fearless hope of inheriting a future status with God (8 : 16-17 a) as well. [39] And since we are "fellow-heirs" with Christ, inasmuch as we now suffer with him, we may securely cling to the hope that we also "may be glorified with him" (8 : 17 b). That we now suffer together with Christ, our "fellow-heir," thus instigates and invigorates our hope of participating in the future, final "glory" (see 5 : 2 b) of God together with Christ.

---

[39] The concept of "heir" was used also in relation to the hope we share with Abraham in Rom 4 : 13.

H. **Our Hope for the Future That Will Far Surpass Our Present Sufferings is Absolutely Assured: Rom 8 : 18-39**

Paul initiates this final, climactic section of Rom 5 – 8 with a bold and encouraging expression of his own convinced hope that the future glory of God will follow the present sufferings of Christians. His strong "conviction" (*logizomai*)[40] accentuates the certainty of the hope that since we Christians necessarily and inevitably suffer with Christ, we will indeed likewise be glorified with him (8 : 17 b). But even more important, Paul's absolute "conviction" emphatically introduces the statement of hope that serves as the thesis or superscription for the rest of this section of the letter, namely, that the future glory which God will reveal to us cannot be compared to, that is, it will more than compensate for and far surpass, the sufferings we presently experience (8 : 18). And Paul begins his eloquent illustration of this unsurpassed greatness of what we hope for by pointing to the intensely longing hope for God's future that is now evident in all of creation.

So great is "the coming glory to be revealed to us" (8 : 18) that even creation has an "eager expectation" (*apokaradokia*)[41] which "awaits" (*apekdechetai*)[42] this future "revelation of the sons of God" (8 : 19). Creation's "eager expectation" and "awaiting" illustrate the intensely expectant, forward-looking and eager character of a hope intent upon the future of God.[43] Creation has an eager expectation which awaits the future glory of God because, although God subjected creation to "futility" or "nothingness" (*mataiotēti*),[44] which was not creation's own doing but "because of the one who

---

[40] We translate *logizomai* here as "I am convinced," although it often has a more weakened sense of "consider," "think," "be of the opinion" or "reckon"; see BAGD, 475-476. On its stronger sense here and elsewhere in Paul, see H. W. Heidland, "*logizomai*," *TDNT* 4 (1967) 288. For Cranfield (*Romans*, 408) *logizomai* in 8 : 18 denotes a "firm conviction"; Schlier (*Römerbrief*, 256) translates it by "ich bin überzeugt" (I am convinced).

[41] BAGD, 92; G. Bertram, "*Apokaradokia*," *ZNW* 49 (1958) 264-270; D. R. Denton, "*Apokaradokia*," *ZNW* 73 (1982) 138-140; as G. Delling ("*apokaradokia*," *TDNT* 1 (1964) 393) states: "Linked with *elpis* in Phil. 1 : 20, the word expresses confident expectation; the *elpis* denotes well-founded hope and the *apokaradokia* unreserved waiting."

[42] As W. Grundmann ("*apekdechomai*," *TDNT* 2 (1964) 56) states: "In the NT *apekdechomai*, as distinct from *ekdechomai* "to wait for someone," is used by Paul to express "expectation of the end."

[43] Paul combines "eager expectation" (*apokaradokia*) and "await" (*apekdechetai*) elsewhere to likewise express the intense expectation and eagerness of eschatological hope; see 1 Cor 1 : 7; Phil 1 : 20; 3 : 20; Gal 5 : 5.

[44] On *mataiotēs* as expressing creation's destiny to unreality or nothingness, a fail-

subjected,"[45] he did so "*in hope*" (*eph' helpidi*) (8 : 20). And there is an "in hope" aspect of creation's subjection to futility because even creation itself *will be freed* from its slavery to corruption to participate in the glorious, future freedom of the children of God (8 : 21). If God himself "*will free*" (*eleutherōthēsetai*, divine passive) creation from its "slavery to corruption," that is, from the consequence of its subjection to futility, then there is truly an "in hope" aspect to creation's subjection. Although God subjected creation to futility in the past, in the future he "will free" creation from this slavish subjection, so that creation eagerly expects and awaits this future freedom "in hope". Creation's hope for God's glorious, future freedom, then, bolsters Paul's conviction that the coming glory of God will far exceed our present sufferings. That "even creation itself" will participate in the future, final freedom which God will establish and reveal to us illustrates the unsurpassed greatness of God's "coming glory"—it extends to and embraces "*even creation itself*!" (8 : 21).

As we Christians well know, "all creation groans together and is in travail together until now" (8 : 22). "Groan together" (*systenazei*) and "be in travail together" (*synōdinei*) further describe the "eager expectation" and forward-looking "awaiting" aspects of creation's hope, but with the connotations of painful suffering, oppression or distress, in accord with creation's having been subjugated to futility and thus enslaved to corruption.

The "groaning together" of all creation expresses a lamentful sighing because of some undesirable circumstance.[46] The undesirable circumstance is creation's subjection to futility. But this "groaning," which often describes or accompanies prayers of lament, has a future orientation, as it expresses a longing or yearning to be freed from present distress in the future.[47] As a

---

ure to achieve its original God-given purpose or "glory," see H. R. Balz, *Heilsvertrauen und Welterfahrung. Strukturen der paulinischen Eschatologie nach Römer 8,18-39* (BEvT 59; Munich: Kaiser, 1971) 39-40; Schlier, *Römerbrief,* 260-261; O. Bauernfeind, "*mataios*," *TDNT* 4 (1967) 523.

[45] This probably refers to Adam as the representative of mankind. See Gen 3 : 15-19; and for the various Jewish traditions regarding Adam's or mankind's role in the "subjection" of creation, see Balz, *Heilsvertrauen,* 41-45; Wilckens, *Römer,* 2. 154; Schlier, *Römerbrief,* 261; Kuss, *Römerbrief,* 626-636.

[46] In the OT *stenazō* refers to deep distress of spirit which can take the form of a prayer of lament to God or accompany prayer. A particularly enlightening example of the close connection between *stenazō* and praying in the OT occurs in Tob 3:1 S: "and groaning (*stenaxas*) I wept and began to pray with groans (*stenagmōn*)." See J. Schneider, "*stenazō*," *TDNT* 7 (1971) 600.

[47] Schneider, "*stenazō*," 601: "Sighing takes place by reason of a condition of oppression under which man suffers and from which he longs to be free because it is not in accord with his nature, expectations, or hopes."

longing or yearning for the future, then, this "groaning" expresses hope. The "groaning" of all creation is a striving forward to God's future glory, previously stated as the "glorious freedom of the children of God" (8 : 21).

All of creation's groaning together is reinforced by its "being in travail together," an expression of intense suffering or agony, as in the process of giving birth. There are Jewish OT and apocalyptic traditions in which "birth-pangs" refer to the sufferings or "woes" out of which the messianic age is given birth. Just as for "groaning," there is an inherent expectation and future orientation to this "travailing," as it looks forward to the end of present pain in the joy of the future "birth".[48] The "travailing together" of all creation then is a present suffering, a straining forward, which looks to the future, final glory of God, and so is likewise an expression of hope.

All creation was subjected to futility in the past and is still presently groaning together and in travail together even "until now" (8 : 22). Since this groaning and travailing of all creation expresses a present suffering which is at the same time an expectant hope looking forward to God's future liberation from this suffering (8 : 21), it further supports Paul's conviction that the sufferings of the present time will be far surpassed by the future glory of God. In other words, if the sure hope for God's future freedom from futility is already inherent in the present suffering of "*all*" creation, then certainly God's hoped-for glory to come will far exceed these present sufferings (8 : 18).

Thus, Paul proclaims that all of creation hopes. Because creation has been subjugated to futility (8 : 20), this hope takes the form of an "eager expectation" which "awaits" (8 : 19) in "groaning and travailing" (8 : 22). Hence, this hope is a kind of suffering in hope, a hopeful suffering, a painful striving and straining beyond itself for God's final freedom from futility. How great must the future glory of God be then (8 : 18), if *all* of creation even *until now* "groans and travails" in hope of it!

Not only is all creation now groaning together in hope, but even "we ourselves," we Christians, intensely "groan" (*stenazomen*) within ourselves, because we possess the "first-fruits" of the Spirit (8 : 23). Already having the Spirit as the "first-fruits," that is, a first installment which guarantees a future completion, assures the attainment of the future goal toward which our "groaning " is directed.[49] The indwelling of the Spirit (8 : 9-11) as "first-

---

[48] BAGD, 793, 895; G. Bertram, "*ōdin*," *TDNT* 9 (1974) 667-674; Balz, *Heilsvertrauen*, 52-54; Schlier, *Römerbrief*, 263. Cranfield, *Romans*, 416 n. 2: "The metaphor is a very natural one to express the thought of severe distress from which a happy and worthwhile issue is to be looked for."

[49] On the significance of "first-fruits" (*aparchē*) and on "Spirit" (*pneumatos*, 8 : 23) as an epexegetical, rather than partitive, genitive in apposition to "first-fruits,"

fruits" thus contributes to the certainty of our "groaning" as an expression of hope. Like the hopeful groaning of all creation our interior groaning as Christians includes an expectant quality which looks forward to God's future salvation: "we groan within ourselves eagerly awaiting (*apekdechomenoi*) sonship, the redemption of our body" (8 : 23 b). This "sonship" refers to the decisive and definitive fulfillment of the sonship we Spirit-gifted Christians already claim (8 : 14-17). It corresponds to the "revelation of the *sons* of God" for which creation awaits in hope (8 : 19). In apposition to this "sonship," "the redemption of our body" further expresses God's future salvation which we Christians "await". It refers to God's final liberation of our mortal bodies in whom the Spirit now dwells (8 : 11). This "redemption" thus corresponds to the "glorious freedom of the children of God," the future goal of creation's hope (8 : 21).

Just as in the hope of all creation (8 : 19-22) so there is a "groaning" or suffering aspect in Christian hope (8 : 23). Our hope as Christians who have received the Spirit takes the form of an inner, lamentful "groaning," that is, a hopeful *suffering* or a *suffering* hope, because of the inevitable sufferings of this present eschatological age (8 : 18), and because of the mortal condition of our bodily existence (8 : 11.23), not yet fully and finally "redeemed" (8 : 23) or "liberated" (8 : 21). But this interior "groaning" is at the same time a *hopeful* suffering or a suffering *hope* because we Christians already possess God's Spirit as the "first-fruits" which guarantees the future completion of the salvation we Christians "await" even as we "groan" (8 : 23).

We Christians expectantly groan for future salvation, because, as Paul continues, "in hope (*elpidi*) we were saved" (8 : 24 a). In other words, we were saved so that we are now in a situation of hope; we were saved so that we can and must exhibit an attitude of hope; we were saved so that now we are open to an unseen and yet to be revealed future salvation. In definition-like style Paul proceeds to describe the future goal of our hope: "Now hope (*elpis*) that is seen is not hope (*elpis*). For who hopes (*elpizei*) for what he sees" (8 : 24 b)? If the goal of hope is something that can be seen, that is, if it partakes of this earthly, human, physically visible realm, then it cannot be a true goal of the hope we Christians can claim. Our hope looks forward not to what is presently visible but to the future, invisible, divine realm.

Light is shed on the meaning of what is "seen" as opposed to what is "unseen" as the future goal of hope, by Paul's statement in a similar context of hope in 2 Cor 4 : 18: "Because we look not to the things that are seen but to the things that are unseen; for the things that are seen are transient, but the things that are unseen are eternal." These transient "things that are

---

see Schlier, *Römerbrief,* 637-638; BAGD, 81; Balz, *Heilsvertrauen,* 56; G. Delling, "*archō,*" *TDNT* 1 (1964) 485-486.

seen" characterize the short time of affliction in 2 Cor 4 : 17, which is effect-
ing an "eternal" weight of "glory" beyond all comparison, characterized by
the "eternal things that are unseen." Thus, the "things that are seen" relate
to the sufferings of this present age; and the "things that are unseen" relate
to the future, eternal glory of God. The ideas and context of hope in 2 Cor
4 : 17-18 closely approximate Rom 8 : 18.23-25, in which Paul likewise describes the hope of Christians for the coming glory of God which will far
surpass present sufferings (compare Rom 8 : 18 with 2 Cor 4 : 17). As in 2
Cor 4 : 17-18, then, the things that we now see (Rom 8 : 24) embrace the
sufferings of this present time (8 : 18) and thus are in no way the goal of our
hope.[50]

As Paul continues to proclaim, "but if we hope (*elpizomen*) for what we
do not see, we eagerly await (*apekdechometha*) with steadfastness (*di' hypo-
monēs*)" (8 : 25). The true goal of our hope, then, is "what we do not see,"
the future, eternal, invisible glory of God. As the goal of our hope, "what
we do not see" further describes and explains the sonship and redemption for
which we groan and await (8 : 23). And just as "what we do not see" corresponds to the "coming glory to be revealed to us," so also "with steadfastness" corresponds to the "sufferings of the present time" (8 : 18). We Christians can eagerly await what we do not see "with steadfastness," with an
attitude of active, persevering endurance over and against the "sufferings of
the present time,"[51] because the unseen, future glory of God for which we
hope (8 : 25) will abundantly exceed any sufferings we presently encounter
(8 : 18).

In sum, because we Christians have already received the indwelling gift
of the Spirit in this time of necessary and inevitable sufferings (8 : 18), we
"groan" within ourselves, lamentfully longing and yearning, as we "await"
God's future and final liberation of our presently oppressive existence (8 : 23).
But because of the overwhelming greatness of the "unseen" future glory of
God for which we, who have already been saved, can and must now hope
(8 : 24-25 a), we do indeed hope as we "eagerly await" this future of God
"with steadfastness" against present sufferings (8 : 25 b).

Precisely because the goal of our hope is the unseen (8 : 25 a), future glory of God (8 : 18), we do not know how to pray for it (8 : 26). But the Spirit
who dwells within us (8 : 9-11.23) helpfully intercedes for us with "wordless

---

[50] The reference to "groaning" (*stenazomen*) for the future heavenly dwelling of
God in 2 Cor 5 : 2.4 is also similar to the "groaning" in Rom 8 : 23; and there is a
similar function for the Spirit: a "guarantee" (*arrabōna*) of future glory in 2 Cor 5 : 5
and the "first-fruits" of future glory in Rom 8 : 23. See Balz, *Heilsvertrauen*, 64-65.

[51] Hauck, "*hypomenō*," 586: "In most of the NT passages *hypomenein* refers to
the steadfast endurance of the Christian under the difficulties and tests of the present
evil age."

groanings" (8 : 26).   That these groanings are wordless and inexpressible ren-
ders them appropriate intercessions for the "unseen" future of God.[52]   As
interior "groanings" of the Spirit they thus accompany our "groaning" within
ourselves, likewise instigated by the Spirit (8 : 23).   God, who searches hearts,
our interior, understands these wordless groanings; he knows the "aspiration"
of the Spirit, for it is according to the will of God that the Spirit intercedes
for us "holy ones" (8 : 27).[53]   Thus, the Spirit assists our "praying," as part
of our hope, with interior "groanings" in accord with the future completion
of God's will, the unseen, future glory of God for which we hope (8 : 25 a),
but which is so great and unsurpassable (8 : 18) that we do not even know
how to pray for it (8 : 26).

But praying or the future goal of our hope becomes a possibility within
our attitude of hope because the Spirit helps and intercedes for us.   The
Spirit's intercession assures that our praying accords with our future hope.   If
the Spirit intercedes with our praying as we await with steadfastness (8 : 25-
26), then we are even more certain that we will attain the unseen, future goal
of our hope (8 : 25 a) and that its glory will far surpass our present sufferings
(8 : 18).

With an encouraging and spirited confessional proclamation (8 : 28-30)
Paul strengthens the previous expressions of Christian hope as he inserts our
attainment of hope's future goal into the certainty of God's eternal plan of
salvation.   That we will arrive at the future goal of our hope is absolutely
assured by God himself: First, we know that God makes everything work
together for the "good," that is, for final salvation or glory,[54] for us who love
God and are called in accord with his purpose (8 : 28; 1 : 6-7).   God guarantees our participation in the completion of his salvific purpose.   Secondly,
from the beginning of his plan of salvation, God has predestined us "to be
conformed to the image of his Son," that is, to participate in the future, final
glory of the risen, heavenly Christ, and so to be among the many brothers of
his first-born Son (8 : 29; 8 : 14-17).   And thirdly, God will surely bring to
final glorification us Christians whom he has already predestined, called and
justified (8 : 30).   It has already been definitively decided within God's eternal plan of salvation, as a process which has already commenced and will
inevitably reach its conclusion.   That God will finally glorify us emphatically

---

[52] See also 2 Cor 12 : 4; Balz, *Heilsvertrauen,* 77-80.   These interior, wordless
groanings should not be equated with glossolalia; see Wilckens, *Römer,* 2. 161 n. 712;
A. J. M. Wedderburn, "Romans 8.26—Towards a Theology of Glossolalia?," *SJT* 28
(1975) 369-377; E. Vallauri, "I gemiti dello Spirito Santo (Rom. 8,26 s.)," *RivB* 27
(1979) 95-113.

[53] On the "aspiration" (*phronēma*) of the Spirit, see Rom 8 : 5-7; in 8 : 6 the
phronēma of the Spirit is the hope for eschatological "life" and "peace".

[54] Schlier, *Römerbrief,* 270.

climaxes the "gradatio" expressing God's activity from the beginning to the end of his total plan of salvation.[55]　Hence, that God "has glorified" us guarantees our participation in the coming "glory" to be revealed to us, which will far surpass the sufferings of the present (8 : 18), so that we can indeed "eagerly await it with steadfastness" (8 : 25).

With the question, "what then shall we say in view of these things?," Paul breaks out with an exuberant salvo (8 : 31-39) which caps off and culminates all that he has previously proclaimed in Rom 5 – 8.　Paul unabashedly asks, "if God is for us, who is against us?" (8 : 31 b), and then assertively reminds us that God did not spare his own Son but gave him up in death "for us" all (8 : 32 a).　This convincing proof that God is "for us" provides the stalwart foundation for our firm hope that God surely "*will* give" us, together with his Son, "all things," the totality and completion of God's future, decisive salvation (8 : 32 b).　"All things" succinctly sums up Paul's previous expressions of hope's future goal (8 : 18.19.21.23.25.28).

Any possible answer that could be given to the question, "who will bring a charge against God's elect (Christians)?,"[56] Paul supersedes with the vigorous protestation that "it is God who justifies!" (8 : 33).[57]　Likewise, no one will condemn us, because Christ who died and was raised now sits at the right hand of God interceding "for us!" (8 : 34).　Paul pointedly proves that God is "for us" (8 : 31 b), then, not only by the *past* death of Christ "for us" (8 : 32 a), but also by his *present* intercession "for us" (8 : 34 b).　Thus, our hope that God *will give* us "everything" (8 : 32 b), the totality of his future salvation, is assured not only because God shows that he is "for us" in the past death of his Son (8 : 31 b-32 a), but also because Christ presently intercedes at the right hand of God "for us" (8 : 34).

Our conclusive hope that nothing can be "against us" since God is "for us" (8 : 31-34) proceeds to that of nothing being able to "separate us" from the "love" of Christ and God (8 : 35-39).　As Paul boldly and brazenly queries, who will separate us from the love of Christ (8 : 35 a) evident not only in his past death for us but still operative through his present intercession for us

---

[55] On the rhetorical device of "gradatio," see Lausberg, *Rhetorik,* § 619, 623, 653, 451.

The aorist *edoxasen,* "he glorified," in 8 : 30 expresses an action from the viewpoint of God's decision or plan to glorify.　The aspect is the eternal plan or purpose of God.　On the "aspect" of Greek verbs, see Zerwick, *Biblical Greek,* § 240-242.

[56] Christians are God's chosen or "elect" (*eklektōn*) in 8 : 33 a and "called" by God in 8 : 30 (*ekalesen*) and 8 : 28 (*klētois*); see also 1 : 6-7.

[57] Although some take 8 : 33 b and 34 b to be questions (e.g., Schlier, *Römerbrief,* 275), translating as statements makes them stronger and more appropriate to the context.　See Balz, *Heilsvertrauen,* 116; Kuss, *Römerbrief,* 650; Wilckens, *Römer,* 2. 170; Cranfield, *Romans,* 434; Michel, *Römer,* 278, 281; Käsemann, *Romans,* 245.

at the right hand of God? Paul continues the question with a seven member enumeration of terms dramatically describing our ever-present suffering situation (8 : 35 b), which he interprets as a "being killed" in fulfillment of God's will as stated in Ps 44 : 22 : "For your sake we are being killed all the day; we have been regarded as sheep for slaughter" (8 : 36).[58] "For your sake" emphasizes that it is for the sake of God and Christ that we Christians suffer and die and not because of any guilt on our part. This suffering cannot possibly "separate" us from the love of God and Christ, on the contrary, since it is humbly endured out of love *for* God (see 8 : 28), it unites us even closer to the love of God and Christ.

Paul then energetically exclaims the hope we cling to in the midst of all our sufferings, a hope solidly grounded upon the love of God and Christ from which we cannot be separated: "But in all these things we are more than triumphing[59] through him who loved us" (8 : 37). This "triumphing" or "overcoming" expresses hope since it is oriented to the future of God and implicitly promises our participation in the final triumph or victory of "he who loved us". That we are "more than triumphing" means we are marching our way to the future, final victory of God.[60] Paul reinforces the certainty of this hope with his personal "conviction" (*pepeismai*) that nothing *will ever be able* to separate us from the powerful love of God in Christ. Here Paul boldly broadens the horizon of our hope to utter extremes. Not only our present sufferings (8 : 18.35) and our "being killed" (8 : 36) but any other power that can be named within all of creation — death, life, angels, principalities, things to come, powers, height, depth, or *any other creature* — will ever be able to separate us from the firm foundation of our hope, the love of God in Christ. Paul's confident hope that nothing will ever separate us from the love of God in Christ (8 : 38-39) adds absolute assurance to his convinced hope that the coming glory to be revealed to us will far exceed our present sufferings (8 : 18).

With regard to hope in 8 : 18-39, we have seen that: 1) Hope extends to all of creation in the form of an eager expectation which awaits the future revelation of God's glory (8 : 19). Having been subjected to futility "in hope" (8 : 20), all creation now groans and is in travail together (8 : 22), as it thus suffers in hope, striving and straining beyond itself for God's future and final freedom from futility (8 : 21).

---

[58] On the relation of what is written in the scriptures to Christians now living in the eschatological age, see 1 Cor 9 : 9-10; 10 : 7-11; Rom 15 : 4. And on Paul's use of LXX Ps 43 : 23 in 8 : 36, see Michel, *Römer*, 283; Kuss, *Römerbrief*, 655.

[59] The unusual expression *hypernikōmen*, "we are more than triumphing," is a Pauline expanded form of *nikaō*, "to triumph" or "win a victory."

[60] O. Bauernfeind, "*nikaō*," *TDNT* 4 (1967) 945: "The word *nikaō* is in the NT a word of promise, an eschatological word."

2) The Spirit serves as a stimulus for our hope in the midst of sufferings. We Christians in whom the Spirit dwells, like creation, suffer in hope as we groan within ourselves awaiting future sonship, God's final liberation from suffering (8 : 23). We were saved "in hope" (8 : 24 a), so that we can and must have an attitude of hope for the future completion of this salvation. And since we hope for the unseen, future glory of God (8 : 24 a), which will far surpass present sufferings (8 : 18), we eagerly await God's future with steadfastness over and against our sufferings (8 : 25 b).

3) Praying is part of our attitude of hope. But we can pray for the unseen, future glory of God as we await it with steadfastness (8 : 25), only because the Spirit dwelling within us intercedes for us with "wordless groanings," assuring that our present praying in hope accords with the incomparable and unsurpassable future goal of hope (8 : 26-27).

4) The attainment of hope's future object, our glorification by God, is a certainty within God's eternal plan of salvation (8 : 28-30).

5) The love of God for us in the death of his Son assures that he will give us the total and complete future salvation for which we hope (8 : 31-32). The intercessory activity of the risen and exalted Christ "for us" (8 : 34) strengthens this assurance and makes even more certain our hope for God's future.

6) In the midst of our sufferings and dying for the sake of God (8 : 35-36), our hope becomes a "more than triumphing," as we are on our way to the final victory over all our sufferings through God who loved us (8 : 37). The love of God in the death of his Son and in Christ's present intercession "for us" is thus, like the Spirit dwelling within us, a most secure foundation for our attitude of hope.

7) As proclamations of hope, Paul's own confident convictions (8 : 18.38-39) strengthen and encourage the hope he proclaims together with his fellow Christians (8 : 23-37), so that we Christians can truly "await with steadfastness" (8 : 25) the coming glory which, according to Paul's own conviction, will far surpass our present sufferings (8 : 18).

I. Summary

To summarize, in 5 : 1-11 Paul announced the hope that is integral to and consequent upon our having been justified by faith through the death of Christ (5 : 1-2). In 5 : 12-21 he proclaimed that it is precisely in the midst of the powers of sin and death that we may claim the sure hope for God's future eternal life, a hope that far surpasses the hopelessness of sin and death. In 6 : 1-14 he demonstrated that we have the possibility to already live, as part of hope, the future life for which we hope. In 6 : 15-23 he exhorted us about the absolute necessity to live this new life of hope now; we not only *can* but *must* "live" this hope. In 7 : 1-6 he gave the further reason why we can and must hope: we have already been freed from hopelessness under the Law. For, as explained in 7 : 7-25, the good Law of God has been transformed by the power of sin into the "Law" of sin which offers only the despairing finality of death. But, as shown in 8 : 1-17, for us who are in Christ Jesus through baptism there is now a "Law" of the Spirit of life which brings us the hope for God's future, final life. And Paul concluded in 8 : 18-39 with enthusiastic enunciations of the unsurpassed greatness and absolute assurance of our new life of hope.

From Rom 5 – 8 we have seen that there are three ingredients involved in the stimulus to hope : the death–resurrection of Christ, the love of God, and the Spirit. These three elements are closely combined in 5 : 5-8: God manifested his own love in the death of Christ for us (5 : 8); this love is presently poured out into our hearts through the Holy Spirit given to us (5 : 5 b). And this guarantees the certainty and reliability of our hope, so that "hope does not shame" (5 : 5 a). These same elements are expressed separately and developed differently in Rom 8. The Spirit of sonship that we have received (8 : 15) dwells *within us* (8 : 9-11; "into our hearts" in 5 : 5 b) and thus provokes our hopeful groaning *within ourselves* as we await future and final sonship (8 : 23). The Spirit likewise secures the praying aspect of our hope, as it intercedes for us according to God so that our praying accords with hope's goal, God's future (8 : 26-27). As in 5 : 5-8 so in 8 : 31-32 God shows that he is "for us" in the death of his own Son "for us" all and this solidly supports our hope that God *will give* us "everything". That "we are more than triumphing," an expression of our hope in the midst of sufferings, is guaranteed by "him who loved us" (8 : 37). And this love of God for us, as manifested in the death of Christ, who was raised and is now at the right hand of God interceding for us (8 : 34), remains so great and powerful that it sustains Paul's confident hope that nothing will ever be able to separate us from so great a love (8 : 35.39).

With regard to hope's future goal, the "glory of God" for which we boast in 5 : 2 b is further specified in 8 : 18-39: This coming "glory" to be revealed to us will far exceed the sufferings of the present (8 : 18); and that God has "glorified" us remains as certain as the climax of his plan of salvation (8 : 28-30). Various aspects of this "glory" are also denoted in 8 : 18-39: "the revelation of the sons of God" (8 : 19), "the freedom of the glory of the children of God" (8 : 21), "sonship, the redemption of our body" (8 : 23), "the things we do not see" (8 : 25), "the good" (8 : 28) and "all things" (8 : 32).

The hope that "we *will* be saved through him (Christ) from the wrath" (5 : 9 b) and that "we *will* be saved by his life" (5 : 10 b), which are based on the love of God in Christ's death for us (5 : 8) find a correspondence in 8 : 18-39. Because Christ died, was raised and now intercedes for us (8 : 34), God "*will* give us all things" (8 : 32 b) and nothing "*will* be able to separate us from the love of God in Christ" (8 : 35.39).

Regarding our present attitude of hope, the idea that suffering causes our hope to take the form of "steadfastness" ultimately leading to a dramatic increase of "hope" (5 : 3-4) finds more illustration and development in 8 : 18-39. So great is the "unseen," coming glory for which we "hope" (8 : 25 a) in the midst of present sufferings (8 : 18), that we await it "with steadfastness" against these sufferings.

Whereas in 5 : 1-11 Paul proclaims mainly the more joyful, "boasting" aspect of hope, so that we even "boast" of sufferings (5 : 3), in 8 : 18-39 he centers more upon the suffering, "groaning" and "eager expectation" aspect of hope (8 : 19-27). His climactic exclamation of the hope that "we are more than triumphing" in all these sufferings in 8 : 37, does, however, offer a correspondence to the three-fold "boasting" in 5 : 2.3.11. In fact, both of these sections climactically conclude on notes of joyful and confident hope in God who loved us in Christ: In 5 : 11 we are "boasting" of God himself through our Lord Jesus Christ; and in 8 : 37-39 we are "more than triumphing" through him who loves us (8 : 37), for Paul is "convinced" that nothing will be able to separate us from the love of God in Christ Jesus our Lord (8 : 38-39).

1. *Our hope as Christians and the hope of Abraham*

The similarity that we have already noted between the hope of Abraham and that of Christians can likewise be seen in 8 : 18-39. Fully aware of the weakness of his human situation, which seemed to contradict God's promise, Abraham was nevertheless strengthened in faith in view of the promise of God, fully convinced that God was able to do what he had promised (4 : 19-21). In other words, Abraham exhibited hope for the future fulfillment of God's promise, despite his present experience of opposition to that promise. Similarly, we Christians, in the midst of the present sufferings of our human situation (8 : 18), nevertheless manifest hope, as we "eagerly await with steadfastness" in the face of these sufferings, since we hope for "what we do not see" (8 : 25), the future glory of God which will far surpass these sufferings (8 : 18). And likewise we display the hope that "we are more than triumphing" (8 : 37) over all of our sufferings through the love of God who will give us "everything" (8 : 32 b). Like Abraham, then, we Christians possess a strong hope in the future of God over and against the sufferings which threaten and oppose hope.

There is also a similarity between Abraham's hopeful "conviction" that God has the "power" to bring to future fulfillment what he promised (4 : 21) and the hopeful conviction of Paul in 8 : 18-39. Like Abraham, Paul is absolutely "convinced" that God will bring about a glory which will supersede weakness and sufferings (8 : 18). And Paul is also "convinced" (8 : 38) that

nothing has the "power" (8 : 39) to separate us from the love of God. In
other words, so powerful is the love of God that Paul is convinced that God
will certainly effect a future and final victory over our sufferings (8 : 35-37).
Both Abraham and Paul, then, had a confidently convinced hope for the
future completion of God's salvific activity.

2. *Paul's purpose of arousing hope in his audience*

The way that Paul strengthens the "we" proclamations of the hope he
shares with his fellow Christians (8 : 23-25.37) by his own proclamations of
hopeful conviction (8 : 18.38-39) illustrates how he continues to impart some
spiritual gift to his listeners in Rome that they might be strengthened and
mutually encouraged with him through their mutual faith, both theirs and his
(1 : 11-12). By these mutual "we" proclamations of hope Paul illustrates how
his fellow Christians, including those in Rome, may be strengthened and
encouraged by the hope which results from their justification by faith. Paul
thus arouses the hope of his listeners by proclamations intended to embrace
them, namely, that "we" have been saved in hope (8 : 24 a) so that "we"
eagerly await with steadfastness the unseen glory for which "we" hope
(8 : 25), and in the midst of sufferings "we" are more than triumphing
(8 : 37).

Paul began to stimulate hope in his audience by his own confident confession of hope in 1 : 16, "for I am not ashamed of the gospel, for it is the
power of God to salvation for all who believe." As an expression of hope in
God's ultimate salvation for us, Paul's personal conviction in 1 : 16 corresponds to those in 8 : 18, "for I am conviced that the sufferings of the present time are not comparable to the coming glory to be revealed to us," and
in 8 : 38-39, "for I am convinced that... (nothing) will be able to separate
us from the love of God in Christ Jesus our Lord." And both 1 : 16 and
8 : 38-39 involve hope in the "power" of God to bring us to future and final
salvation. In 1 : 16 the gospel of which Paul is not ashamed is the "power"
(*dynamis*) of God for salvation" and in 8 : 38-39 the love of God is so powerful that Paul is convinced that nothing "will be able" (*dynēsetai*), that is,
have the "power," to separate us from it. Thus, the hope that we Christians
can and must live now is absolutely assured by God himself.

In sum, Paul began the letter proper with his own confession of hope
(1 : 16-17), which reached a first climax in the hope of Abraham as a consequence of justification by faith (4 : 13-25), which, in turn, progressed to the
hope of justified Christians (5 : 1-11) over and against former hopelessness
under the powers of sin, death and Law (5 : 12 – 8 : 17) and reached a second
climax in the absolutely assured, triumphant hope that Paul shares with his
fellow Christians (8 : 18-39).

Chapter V

The Hope for All Israel: Rom 9 : 1 – 11 : 36

Although we can consider Rom 9 – 11 as a unity separate from the previous unity of Rom 1 – 8, these chapters are by no means merely an excursus within the letter. We propose that they are essential especially to the theme of hope that pervades and that is part of Paul's intention for the letter. The situation in which most of Israel, God's specially privileged people, does not believe in the gospel about the Christ who has come from Israel (9 : 5) is most crucial to the hope of Christians. It calls into question the power of the gospel (see 1 : 16 b) and of the word of God (9 : 6 a) as the valid basis for a universal hope. If the word of God has not brought Israel as a people to faith in their own Messiah, how can Christians base their hope upon God's word in the gospel about his Son (see 1 : 2-4)? What role, then, does Israel's failure to believe play with regard to the hope of Christians?

Paul dramatically develops a hope for Israel as follows:[1] A) First, he communicates his great concern that Israel has failed to believe and have the new hope (9 : 1-5). B) But he shows how within God's sovereign will there is still hope for Israel (9 : 6-29). C) To have this hope all Israel must do is believe (9 : 30 – 10 : 21). D) Paul illustrates how crucially important the situation of Israel is for Christian hope (11 : 1-24). E) And finally, he climactically proclaims the hope that "all Israel will be saved!" (11 : 25-36).

A. Paul's Concern for His Fellow Israelites Who Have the Basis But Not the Attitude of the New Hope: Rom 9 : 1-5

The "deep sorrow" and "unceasing anguish" of heart (9 : 2) that Paul feels because of the situation of unbelieving Israel carries the intense *seriousness* of a truth spoken "in Christ" and borne witness by his conscience "in the Holy Spirit" (9 : 1). Paul is so earnestly worried about the welfare of his fellow Israelites that he entertains the astounding and sincerely meant but impossible wish to separate himself from Christ for their sake (9 : 3). Paul

[1] M. Zerwick, "Drama populi Israel secundum Rom 9-11," *VD* 46 (1968) 321-338.

would do anything he could to bring unbelieving Israel to faith in the gospel. Their situation remains all the more unbearable and anguishing for Paul *since* they have the God-given, salvation-historical prerogative of being named "Israelites" (see Gen 32 : 28), who possess such traditional privileges as "the sonship," "the glory," "the covenants," "the giving of the Law," "the worship," "the promises" and "the patriarchs" (9 : 4-5). And what is more, by way of climax to all these privileges, it is from the "Israelites" that the Messiah, "the Christ" came with regard to his human descent (9 : 5). Despite this impressive list of privileges providing a God-given basis for Israel's hope for the eschatological blessings of God,[2] Israel as a whole has not believed in God's gospel about the Christ, which fulfills the hope of these privileges.[3]

But since these God-given privileges still serve as a stimulus for hope and still belong to the "Israelites," they imply a hope for unbelieving Israel, a hope which Paul makes more explicit in what follows.

B. Within God's Sovereign Will There is Still Hope for Israel: Rom 9 : 6-29

That Israel as such has not believed in the Messiah does not mean that "the word of God" has "fallen away" or "failed" (*ekpeptōken*) (9 : 6 a). God's word, his purpose and promise for salvation, remains valid and operative even now.[4] And if this is so, then the word of God still provides a valid basis of hope not only for Christians but for unbelieving Israel.

Paul explains how it is according to "free choice" or "election" (9 : 11) that God fulfills his "word of promise" (9 : 9) and accomplishes his salvific "purpose" (9 : 11). First, God's election is evident in his choice of the line of Isaac (rather than of Ishmael, see Gen 21 : 8-14) to carry the promise and thus the hope that accompanies designation as the "seed" of Abraham. For

---

[2] B. Byrne, '*Sons of God'-'Seed of Abraham*' (AnBib 83; Rome: Biblical Institute, 1979) 128: "... the privileges established through God's acts of grace in the past and especially to be realized in the ideal future state of the nation; it is the language of the 'eschatological blessings'."

[3] See 8 : 14-23 for the Christian hope for "sonship"; 5 : 2 b and 8 : 18 for the hope for "glory"; 8 : 2-4 for the fulfillment of the hope of the Law; 1 : 2-4 on the gospel as the fulfillment of what was "previously *promised*"; 4 : 1-25 for the hope of Abraham who was one of the "patriarchs" (*pateres*, 9 : 5 a), the "forefather" (*propatora*, 4 : 1) of Israel, and is now the "father" (*patros*, 4 : 12) of Christians.

[4] *Ekpeptōken* is in the perfect tense meaning "has not failed (in the past) and still is not failing (in the present)." See Wilckens, *Römer*, 2. 191-192; Schlier, *Römerbrief*, 290.

not all the descendants of Israel constitute the Israel through whom the word of God's promise operates as a basis for hope (9 : 6 b). Nor are all the children (of Abraham) designated the "seed" of Abraham, but, in accord with the hope-bringing promise of Gen 21 : 12, it is "in Isaac (that) there will be called a seed for you" (9 : 7).[5] In other words, not physical descent from Abraham constitutes the children (of Abraham) as the children of God, but the promise of God establishes them as "the children of the promise" who are thereby reckoned (by God) as the "seed" (of Abraham) (9 : 8). The hope for the end-time blessings that accompanies being a "seed" of Abraham depends upon God's promise. For the "word of the promise" granted Sarah (as opposed to Hagar) the hope expressed in Gen 18 : 10.14: "At this time I will return and Sarah will have a son" (9 : 9). Thus, God's word of promise, the basis for hope, did not fail (9 : 6 a) but operated through his election of Sarah and Isaac over Hagar and Ishmael for the promise and thus the hope of being the privileged "seed" of Abraham and "the children of God."

Secondly, God's choice of Jacob over his older brother Esau even more graphically manifested his election. They were both conceived through one and the same act of conception between Rebecca and Isaac (9 : 10), so that they were full, twin brothers with the same mother (unlike the half brothers Isaac and Ishmael). But even before they were born or had done anything good or bad (9 : 11 a), Rebecca was told God's promise of Gen 25 : 23 that "the elder (Esau) will serve the younger (Jacob)" (9 : 12 b), in accord with God's election as written in Mal 1 : 2-3, "Jacob I loved, but Esau I hated" (9 : 13). This happened in order that the salvific "purpose of God" might continue "according to election" (9 : 11 b), and not from any human works or activity but solely from the "one who calls" (9 : 12 a). God's word of promise as a basis for hope, then has not "failed" (9 : 6 a), on the contrary, the purpose of God "continues" so that there is still hope, but it continues according to the free election (9 : 11 b) of the God "who calls" (9 : 12 a). Hope depends not on human activity but on the "calling" of God.

God's election of some over others within Israel provokes the question of whether there is "injustice" or "unfaithfulness" on the part of God, but Paul abruptly dismisses such a thought with a firm "by no means!" (9 : 14). In his absolute freedom and sovereignty God remains totally true to himself, for he says to Moses in Exod 33 : 19, "I will have mercy on whom I have mercy, and I will have compassion on whom I have compassion" (9 : 15).

---

[5] Taking "all the children" (parallel to "all who are from Israel" in 9 : 6 b) as the subject of the grammatically ambiguous clause in 9 : 7 a and "seed of Abraham" (parallel to "seed" in 9 : 7 b) as the predicate preserves the same special meaning for "seed" in both 9 : 7 a and 9 : 7 b. See C. K. Barrett, *A Commentary on the Epistle to the Romans* (HNTC; New York: Harper & Row, 1957) 180-181; M. Black, *Romans* (NCB; London: Oliphants, 1973) 131.

So then, the purpose of God continues according to election (9 : 11 b) and does not depend on human "willing" or "striving," but solely on the sovereign God's "showing of mercy" (9 : 16).[6] As a consequence, hope emerges from the sovereign God who freely shows his mercy, not from human willing or striving.

In carrying out his salvific purpose (9 : 6 a.11 b) according to election God not only has mercy on whomever he "wills" (e.g. on Moses, see Exod 33 : 17-19), but "hardens" whomever he "wills" (e.g. Pharaoh, see Exod 4 : 21; 7 : 3; 9 : 12; 10 : 20; 11 : 10; 14 : 4.17) (9 : 18). Yet even this "hardening" (of the heart) serves God's salvific purpose and thus gives cause for hope. For in God's own words to Pharaoh in Exod 9 : 16, "for this very purpose I have raised you up in order that I might show my power in you, and in order that my name might be proclaimed in all the earth" (Rom 9 : 17). The manifestation of the "power" of God (by saving Israel in the Exodus event) and the proclamation of the "name" of God throughout the world furthers his salvific purpose (9 : 11 b) and fulfills his word (9 : 6 a) even through the "hardening," the negative part of his free election. Whether through mercy or hardening, then, the accomplishment of God's salvific purpose, the foundation for hope, depends upon God's sovereign "will" (9 : 18).

Paul objects—how is it possible for God to still find fault, then, if no one can really resist his sovereign "will" (9 : 19)? In other words, what can one do that is not embraced by God's plan? Even those who seem to resist it (like Pharaoh) actually obey it. Paul overrules this objection with counter questions based on traditional biblical imagery which underlines the absolute authority of the divine creator over his own human creatures: "O mere man, who are you to answer back to God? Will what is molded say to the molder, 'Why have you made me thus?' Or does not the potter have *authority* over the clay, to make from the same lump one vessel for honor and another for dishonor?" (9 : 20-21).[7] As sovereign creator, then, God has the "authority" (9 : 21), the right or freedom of choice, to make his creatures serve different functions in the accomplishment of his salvific purpose (9 : 11 b.6 a). And so there is still hope for both Christians and unbelieving Israel, even though they play different roles in the accomplishment of God's salvific purpose.

Much like Pharaoh (9 : 17), unbelieving Israel plays the role of the "vessels of wrath" (9 :22) in God's salvific purpose : It was God's free and sovereign "will" (9 : 18) to "harden" Pharaoh and thereby continue his salvific

---

[6] Rom 9 : 11 b should be understood as the subject of 9 : 16; see Zerwick and Grosvenor, *Analysis,* 480. Thus, 9 : 16 is a parallel development of 9 : 12 a.

[7] See Isa 29 : 16; 45 : 9; 64 : 7; Wis 12 : 12; 15 : 7; Jer 18 : 6; Job 10 : 9; 33 : 6; Sir 33 : 10-13.

purpose by dramatically "manifesting" his "power" in Pharaoh for the sake of saving the people of God in the Exodus so that the "name" of God, the salvific purpose of God, might be spread throughout all the earth (Exod 9 : 16 in Rom 9 : 17). Similarly, it is now God's sovereign "will" to save his people by "manifesting" his wrath and making known his "power" in enduring with much patience "vessels of wrath," unbelieving Israel, fit for destruction (9 : 22). God's manifestation of his wrath and power in unbelieving Israel continues his salvific purpose as it is oriented to the salvation of those *"called"* to future "glory" as "vessels of mercy," the reconstituted people of God (9 : 23-25).[8] The negative function of unbelieving Israel as "vessels of wrath" fit for destruction (9 : 22), then, has its positive counterpart within God's overall salvific purpose in the function of believing Christians as "vessels of mercy" prepared for God's future "glory" (9 : 23), just as God in creation makes one vessel for the role of "honor" and another for "dishonor" (9 : 21). The situation of unbelieving Israel does not destroy but rather furthers God's salvific purpose (9 : 11 b) so that there is still a firm basis of hope for those who believe in God's unfailing word (9 : 6 a). Furthermore, there exists at least a faint glimmer of hope for unbelieving Israel itself indicated by the expression of God's "enduring" them "with much patience" (9 : 22), which is meant for their conversion (see 2 : 4).

Closely co-ordinated to the "vessels of wrath" within God's salvific purpose are the "vessels of mercy," which represent believing Christians (9 : 23). These "vessels of mercy" show how the salvific purpose of God continues even now by the free and sovereign election of the God who "calls" and "shows mercy" (9 : 6 b-21). It is part of God's salvific will to make known the wealth of his glory upon vessels of mercy, which he prepared beforehand for future glory (9 : 23). God has already "called" "us" Christians, not only from the Jews but also from the Gentiles, to be vessels of his "mercy" (9 : 23; and see 9 : 15.16.18) and thus to have the hope for the future, final "glory" (9 : 23; and see 5 : 2 b; 8 : 17-18, 30) for which God has already prepared us (9 : 24). Our hope is bolstered since our "call" by God fulfills God's own word of promise recorded by the prophet Hosea (2 : 25 and 2 : 1), according to which God would "call" a new people and bestow on them the hope that goes with being "called" the sons of the living God (9 : 25-26). Despite Israel's failure to believe, then, the firm word of God's promise (9 : 6a.25-26) and his salvific purpose (9 : 11 b) has in no way failed but stands as a valid basis of future hope for us Christians whom God has "called" as a new people from both Jews and Gentiles (9 : 24), "vessels of

---

[8] S. Lyonnet (*Quaestiones in Epistulam ad Romanos. Series Altera. Rom 9–11* (3 d ed.; Rome: Biblical Institute, 1975) 60-65) shows how the manifestation of God's wrath and power is oriented to the salvation of his people by citing *Pss. Sol.* 13 : 6-8; 8 : 30-35; Wis 11 : 20-12 : 2; 12 : 10-21; Hos 11 : 8-9.

mercy" with the hope for the future "glory" of God (9 : 23). Thus, Paul has demonstrated that despite the failure of Israel God remains the God of hope for believing Christians—both Jews and Gentiles, but he is the God of hope as the one who "calls" (9:12 a) and "shows mercy" (9 : 16) according to his free and sovereign election.

But what about the future of *unbelieving* Israel, Paul's primary concern here (9 : 1-5)? Is God still the God of hope for Israel? Indeed, for Paul presents the prophetic promise for the future of Israel as stated by Isaiah (10 : 22-23 combined with Hos 2 : 1 a) who even now cries out "on behalf of"[9] Israel, "If the number of the sons of Israel be as the sand of the sea, a remnant will be saved! For, fully completing and firmly establishing[10] (it), the Lord will execute (his) word (of promise) on the earth "[11] (9 : 27-28). The hope that a "remnant" of Israel "will be saved" (*sōthēsetai*) is based upon God's word of promise to Abraham that his descendants would be as numerous "as the sand of the sea."[12] In other words, if the number of (still unbelieving) Israel[13] is to be as numerous as the sand of the sea in accord with God's "word" of promise, which is still operative and effective (9 : 6 a.28), then surely at least[14] a remnant of unbelieving Israel will be

---

[9] The preposition *hyper* in 9 : 27 is not merely the equivalent of *peri* (concerning), but has its ordinary sense of "on behalf of" or "in favor of" when used in reference to persons; see Rom 5 : 6.7.8; 8 : 27.31.32.34; 9 : 3; 10 : 1; 14 : 15; 15 : 30; 16 : 4; and see Lyonnet, *Quaestiones*, 73-74; T. Zahn, *Der Brief des Paulus an die Römer* (KNT 6; 2 d ed.; Leipzig: Deichert, 1910) 466 n. 42.

[10] F. Zorell, *Lexicon Graecum Novi Testamenti* (3 d ed.; Paris: Lethielleux, 1961, reprinted, Rome: Biblical Institute, 1978) 1279: "decido, firmiter statuo"; also Lyonnet, *Quaestiones*, 80.

[11] Lyonnet, *Quaestiones*, 79-80; Zerwick, "Drama populi Israel," 330.

[12] See Gen 22 : 17; 32 : 9-12 (in the mouth of Jacob); see also Gen 13 : 16; 28 : 14 (for the similar expression, "as the sand (dust) of the earth").

"As the sands of the sea" occurs in both LXX Isa 10 : 22 a and LXX Hos 2 : 1 a; but the Pauline quotation replaces "the people of Israel" in Isa 10 : 22 a with "the number of the sons of Israel" from Hos 2 : 1 a, probably to avoid confusion in view of the expressions of "my people" in Rom 9 : 25-26.

See also LXX Dan 3 : 35-36 for another expression of the Abrahamic promise of a seed as numerous as the sand on the seashore.

[13] "Israel" in 9 : 27 undoubtedly refers to unbelieving Israelites, who have not yet been "called" (9 : 24-26) or "saved". Paul uses the term "Jews" to refer to those Israelites who have believed in 9 : 24. That these believing "Jews" are part of a "remnant" of Israel will be expressed later in Rom 11, but in 9 : 27-29 Paul is concerned with the future hope for a remnant from those Israelites who presently do not believe.

[14] Many translate the quote in 9 : 27 as a concessive clause ("although" rather than "if" for *ean*) and add an "only" in the apodosis: "(only) a remnant will be saved." Whatever may be the original sense of Isa 10 : 22 (H. Cazelles ("A propos de quelques

saved. Thus, there is hope that at least some of the unbelieving Israelites, the "vessels of wrath designed for destruction" (9 : 22), will believe and be saved by God. And this hope that "a remnant will be saved" (9 : 27) gains certainty by the assurance that God will ultimately fulfill his "word" (9 : 6a.28) of promise and surely bring his salvific "purpose" (9 : 11 b) to its final and decisive conclusion on earth (9 : 28).

Paul then presents yet further hope for Israel by citing another prophetic passage which applies to Israel's present situation. That which Isaiah (1 : 9) has foretold can now be spoken by unbelieving Israel, "If the Lord of hosts had not left us a seed, we would have become as Sodom and we would have been made like Gomorrah" (9 : 29). The hope represented by a "remnant" is here taken up and developed by the hope representend by a "seed"[15] which God has left for "us," unbelieving Israelites. If God had not left for "us" a seed, then "we" (unbelieving Israel) would have been totally without hope because "we" would have been utterly destroyed like the cities of Sodom and Gomorah (Gen 19 : 24-29). There is thus an added aspect to the hope for unbelieving Israel here. Whereas Paul previously expressed the sure hope that at least a remnant will be saved from the promised great number of Israelites (9 : 27-28), he now expresses the hope that this remnant or seed implies for the non-remnant remainder of unbelieving Israel (9 : 29). In other words, unbelieving Israelites, the "we" who are now the speakers of what was *prophetically* foretold, have the hope that "we" will not suffer final destruction like Sodom and Gomorrah because God has promised to leave "us" a seed or remnant (9 : 27). Hope for a remnant (9 : 27-28) implies and includes hope for the others as well (9 : 29). Thus, there is still hope for Israel, a hope based upon the still effective word of God (9 : 6a.27-29) and his still continuing salvific purpose (9 : 11 b).

To sum up, Paul has demonstrated (1) that hope is ultimately dependent upon the sovereign God who "calls" (9 : 12 a) and "shows mercy" (9 : 16)

---

textes difficiles relatifs à la justice de Dieu dans l'Ancien Testament," *RB* 58 (1951) 176-178) avoids the limiting "only" even for Isa 10 : 22; R. Lack (*La Symbolique du Livre d'Isaïe. Essai sur l'image littéraire comme élément de structuration* (AnBib 59; Rome: Biblical Institute, 1973) 242) regards Isa 10 : 22 as a later addition inspired by Isa 28 : 22; its present reference is to an eschatological remnant.), in the Pauline context it functions as an expression of future hope for unbelieving Israel, not a "limiting" judgment on Israel. We thus follow Lyonnet (*Quaestiones,* 74-80) in considering the quote in 9 : 27 to be an "eventual" conditional clause so that if any word is to be added to the apodosis in 9 : 27, it would be "surely" and/or "at least" rather than "only," thus, "surely at least a remnant will be saved!" See also Zerwick, "Drama populi Israel," 330.

[15] Cranfield, *Romans,* 503: "... (Paul) understood *sperma* in this Isaiah verse simply as a way of expressing the idea of remnant but at the same time focusing attention on the hope for the future attaching to it."

according to his free choice; (2) that therefore the hope of believing Christians, both Jews and Gentiles, remains valid despite the failure of Israel to believe (9 : 22-26); and (3) that there is still hope for unbelieving Israel based on God's enduring word and salvific purpose (9 : 6 a, 11 b, 27-29).

C. The Hope Based on Faith is Still Available to a Disobedient Israel: Rom 9 : 30 – 10 : 21

Whereas Paul previously treated the problem of unbelieving Israel primarily from the side of God (9 : 6-29), he now treats the same problem primarily from the side of Israel (9 : 30 – 10 : 21). And whereas he demonstrated that there is still hope for Israel based on the free calling and mercy of God, he now demonstrates that there is still hope for Israel based on their coming to faith in the gospel.

Paul presents the ironical paradox of Israel's present situation: "What then shall we say? Gentiles who did not pursue righteousness have attained righteousness, the righteousness (that comes) from faith; but Israel who pursued the Law of righteousness did not arrive at the Law!" (9 : 30-31). And what is the reason for this? It is because Israel did not attain righteousness "from faith" but thought "as if" they could attain it "from works" (of the Law) (9 : 32 a). In their failure, then, Israelites "stumbled over the stone of stumbling" (9 : 32 b; see Isa 8 : 14). Thus, they "stumbled over" the very "stone" which, as written in Isa 28 :16, God himself placed in Zion (Israel) to be a basis of hope for those who believe in it. This "stone," which refers to Christ (see 10 : 11), is a "stone of stumbling and rock of offense, but[16] he who believes in it (him)" has the hope that he "*will* not be put to shame" (9 : 33). In other words, although Israel "has stumbled" in not attaining righteousness from faith, the hope that they "will not be put to shame"[17] by God in the final judgment is still available to them in accord with God's own word of promise in Isa 28 : 16, if they only *believe* in God's "stumbling stone," Christ.[18]

---

[16] The "neutral" use of simple *kai* for "but"; see Zerwick, *Biblical Greek*, § 455 β; Lyonnet, *Quaestiones*, 84; Käsemann, *Romans*, 277.

[17] "Not being put to shame" expresses hope in Romans; in 1 : 16 it expresses Paul's confident hope in the gospel and in 5 : 5 Christian "hope does not shame," it is guaranteed by God; see also 6 : 21; Käsemann, *Romans*, 279.

[18] Israel's "stumbling" is thus not a definitive "fall" (see 11 : 11), so that the hope based on faith is still open to them. Paul's inclusion of Isa 28 : 16 b in Rom 9 : 33, then, does not just refer to the Gentiles who have attained righteousness "from faith"

Further disclosing his deep concern for his fellow Israelites (see 9 : 1-3), Paul informs his "brothers," the Christians in Rome, of his personal prayer of hope for Israel: "My heart's desire and prayer to God for them (is) for (their) salvation" (10 : 1). Here Paul states his ardent hope that his fellow Israelites will arrive at "salvation," the same future goal for which Christians hope. [19] But Paul recognizes that although Israelites have a subjective basis for hope because of the "zeal" they have for God, it is defective because it is not directed by the proper knowledge of God (10 : 2). For in seeking to establish their own righteousness, they have not "submitted" themselves in obedient faith to the righteousness of God (10 : 3). For now Christ is the "end" (*telos*), the termination, [20] of the Law because righteousness now comes to all who *believe* (10 : 4). Hence, "believing" in Christ, rather than a "zeal for God" in doing the works of the Law, now provides the proper subjective basis for the hope of God's salvation.

Paul then illustrates how the righteousness based on doing the works of the Law has now been terminated by God's righteousness based on faith in Christ—a faith which God has brought so near that it is readily available to "all" (10 : 4; also 10 : 11.13), including (and especially) unbelieving Israelites. For even Moses warns (in Lev 18 : 5) that in righteousness based on the Law a person has "life" nowhere else but in "doing" the works of the Law. But it is not necessary for anyone to pursue or strive after Christ the way that Israel "pursues" the Law of righteousness (9 : 31), rather, God has already brought him from heaven and raised him from the dead (10 : 6-7). And so, "the word of faith" which "we" (Paul and his fellow Christians) preach, the word which instigates the act of believing, is so near to you that it is already in your mouth and heart (10 : 8). [21] Hence, the faith that now provides the proper subjective basis of hope for salvation is readily available to "all"—and therefore (especially) to Israel.

The hope of participating in God's future and final salvation is based upon the act of believing in Christ which is so near to all. For if you "con-

---

(9 : 30), but contains an appeal for Israel to believe—Israel has stumbled over the stumbling stone, *but* he who *believes* in him will not be put to shame (9 : 32 b-33).

On Paul's combination of Isa 28 : 16 and Isa 8 : 14 in Rom 9 : 33 and the differences from the OT texts, see Wilckens, *Römer*, 2. 213-214; Kuss, *Römerbrief*, 745-747.

[19] On "salvation" as the goal of hope in Romans, see 1 : 16; 5 : 9-10; 8 : 24; 9 : 27; 10 : 9-10.13; 11 : 11.26; 13 : 11.

[20] Michel, *Römer*, 326-327; Schlier, *Römerbrief*, 311; Käsemann, *Romans*, 282-283.

[21] In his exegesis of Deut 30 : 11-14 in Rom 10 : 6-8 Paul transfers the statements about the "commandment" of the Law, which was near and easily available to Israel, to "Christ" and the "word of faith" in Christ. See Schlier, *Römerbrief*, 311-312; Wilckens, *Römer*, 2. 224-227; Lyonnet, *Quaestiones*, 91-106.

fess with your mouth (see 10:8) that Jesus is Lord," and "believe in your heart" (see 10:8) that God raised him from the dead, then you have hope that "you will be saved" by God (10:9). For with the heart a person believes and thus has hope for future righteousness, and with the mouth a person confesses and thus has hope for future salvation (10:10).[22]. And this is precisely the "salvation" (10:1) Paul prays that Israel may likewise hope for by coming to believe in Christ through the word of faith that is so near to all. Paul then repeats his appeal for this faith, but this time introduces it with "everyone"—"*everyone* who believes in him (Christ)" has hope that "he will not be put to shame" (by God) (10:11). This faith and the hope that accompanies it is thus available to "all". For there is no distinction between Jew and Greek; the same Lord is Lord of "all," who makes rich "all" who call upon him (10:12). For, as written in Joel 3:5, "*Everyone* who calls upon the name of the Lord" (in faith) has hope that "he *will* be saved" by God (10:13). Thus, hope for God's future and final "salvation" (10:1.9.10.13) has its subjective basis in the faith that is universally near and easily available to all. The hope for salvation (10:1) is thus still an open possibility for Israel, if they only believe.

Paul underlines faith's nearness and availability to all as he elaborates upon our "preaching" this "word of faith" (see 10:8) to everyone. He lists the necessary ingredients for the chain-like process of coming to faith (and hope): if "all" are to "call upon" the name of the Lord (10:13), they must first "believe"; if they are to "believe," they must first "hear"; if they are to "hear," there must first be a "preacher" (10:14); but before people can "preach" they must first be "sent" to preach by God (10:15 a). But the preachers have indeed been sent and the gospel is now being proclaimed in accord with what was written in Isa 52:7, "How timely[23] are the feet of those who have brought good news of good things (God's end-time salvation)!" (10:15 b). But despite the preachers that have been sent by God, not "all" have "obeyed" by believing in the gospel (10:16 a). So now the lamentful words of Isa 53:1 a apply to the present preachers of the gospel, "Lord, who has believed in hearing us?" (10:16 b).[24] And so we see again that "faith" stems from "hearing," and "hearing" ensues from the "word of

---

[22] Both "righteousness" and "salvation" in 10:10 express the goal of hope in terms of God's future eschatological salvation. See Schlier, *Römerbrief,* 314; Michel, *Römer,* 331.

[23] *Hōraioi* is best translated "timely," in reference to the moment of eschatological timeliness; see BAGD, 896; Schlier, *Römerbrief,* 317; Käsemann, *Romans,* 294; Wilckens, *Römer,* 2. 228.

[24] We take *akoē* here and in 10:17 to be the act of hearing or listening with *hēmōn* as objective genitive, so that it accords with the verbs for "hearing" in 10:14. 18; see BAGD, 30.

Christ," that is, the "word" in which Christ himself speaks and acts (10 : 17). But Paul emphatically insists that those who do not yet believe do in fact already have this necessary prerequisite for believing—they all "have heard" the "word of Christ." For the words of Ps 19 : 4 now apply to those who are preaching the gospel, the word of Christ: "Their voice has gone out to all the earth, and their words to the ends of the world" (10 : 18). Hence, the necessary prerequisites for believing—the preaching and hearing by all of the word of Christ—are even now fulfilled, so that those (especially Israel) who have not yet "obeyed" or believed (10 : 16) in the gospel still have every possibility to believe and call upon the name of the Lord in order to have the hope that they "will be saved" (10 : 13-14).

Paul then returns explicitly to "Israel" and the paradox of Gentiles coming to faith in the Messiah before Israel as a whole. He maintains that Israel already knew (10 : 19 a) that Gentiles would come to faith ahead of them. First of all, God already promised Israel through Moses in Deut 32 : 21 b that "I will make you jealous of a non-nation; of a non-understanding nation I will make you angry" (10 : 19 b).[25] Here we have an indication of the interrelationship in God's plan between the belief of Gentiles and the unbelief of Israel. It is in fulfilling this promise of God by becoming "jealous" of the faith of the "non-understanding," "non-nation" Gentiles that Israel can come to faith (see 11 : 11.14).[26] And there is now reason for Israel to become "jealous" of the Gentiles because the words of God himself that Isaiah dared to speak (Isa 65 : 1) have now been fulfilled in the Gentiles' coming to faith prior to Israel: "I have been found by those not seeking me; I have shown myself to those not asking for me" (10 : 20). But in Isa 65 : 2 God even now pleads before Israel: "All day long I stretch out my hands to a disobedient and contrary people" (10 : 21). Hence, there is still hope from God's side in that he constantly and continually ("all day long")[27] extends his hands to unbelieving Israel.

The people of Israel have had and still have every opportunity to believe and thus have hope for God's salvation: there is the appeal for "he (everyone) who believes" in the "stumbling stone" (Isa 28 : 16 b in 9 : 33; 10 : 11); although it is a defective zeal, Israel nevertheless has a "zeal for God"

---

[25] Paul has *hymas* (you) in both places where LXX Deut 32 : 21 b has *autous* (them); he thus applies the words of God more directly to "you," Israel.

[26] That God "will make (Israel) jealous" of the Gentiles does not describe Israel's present situation but is yet to happen in the future (note the future tenses of *parazēlōsō* and *parorgiō*). Against Wilckens (*Römer*, 2. 231) then the motif of making Israel jealous is just as "positive" here in 10 : 19 as in 11 : 11.14. See Schlier, *Römerbrief*, 329.

[27] The Pauline version of Isa 65 : 2 emphasizes the words "all day long" by placing them before the verb, whereas in the OT versions they are after the verb.

(10 : 2); God has brought Christ and faith in him very "near" (10 : 6-8); faith
in Christ is available to "all" (10 : 9-13); the prerequisites of preaching and
hearing the word of Christ have been met for all, including Israel (10 : 14-18);
Israel can now come to faith through "jealosy" of the Gentiles who have
believed ahead of them (10 : 19-20); and God has continually extended an
offer of faith to Israel (10 : 21). The hope based on faith is still available to
a disobedient Israel, but Israel as a whole has, in fact, not yet believed. Will
this unbelief remain permanent and become definitive, or will Israel eventually come to faith?

D. **The Hope of Christians is Interrelated to the Situation of Israel: Rom 11 : 1-24**

Paul returns to the consideration of Israel's unbelief primarily from the
side of God and his salvific plan. He rhetorically queries whether Israel's
continuing unbelief means that God has in fact rejected his people (11 : 1 a).
"By no means!" he obstinately protests, for that would mean God has rejected Paul himself, who stands in solidarity with Israel as "an Israelite from
the seed of Abraham, of the tribe of Benjamin" (11 : 1 b). No, God has not
rejected his people whom he "chose beforehand" (11 : 2 a). There is still
hope from God for Israel, since the scriptural passage about Elijah (1 Kgs
19 : 10-18) now applies to and illustrates the present situation regarding Israel
(11 : 2 b). Elijah's complaint to God against Israel (11 : 2 c) indicated the
hopelessness of Israel's rebellion against God and his prophets: "Lord, they"
(Israel) have killed your prophets, they have destroyed your altars, and I
alone am left, and they seek my life" (1 Kgs 19 : 10.14 in 11 : 3). But God's
reply assures Elijah that there is still hope because God has preserved a remnant for himself: "I have kept for myself seven thousand men, who have not
bowed the knee to Baal" (1 Kgs 19 : 18 in 11 : 4). And so also at the present
time, when Israel as a whole does not believe, there is nevertheless a "remnant" (Christian Jews) "freely chosen by grace" (11 : 5). As in the case of
Elijah, there is still hope for Israel represented by a remnant of believers out
of Israel, but a hope based on God's freely given "grace," not on the
achievement of "works" (of the Law), otherwise "grace" would not be "grace" (11 : 6).

What then does this mean for God's salvific plan?—Israel as a whole did
not obtain what it sought ("righteousness" with God, see 9 : 31); the "elect"
(Christian Jews) did obtain it, but the others (non-Christian Jews) "were hardened" by God (11 : 7). Their "hardening" in unbelief "to this very day"
accords with God's plan to blind their eyes from believing as written in the
scriptures: "God gave them a spirit of stupor (Isa 29: 10), eyes that should
not see and ears that should not hear, to this very day" (Deut 29 : 3; see also

Isa 6 : 10) (11 : 8). And now, also in accord with God's plan revealed in the scriptures, Israel's continual "stumbling" (see 9 : 32-33) into the trap and being "blinded" in unbelief fulfills what David once wished God would do to his enemies in Ps 69 : 23-24: "Let their table become a snare and a trap, a stumbling-stone and a retribution for them; let their eyes be darkened so that they do not see, and bend their backs forever" (11 : 9-10). It is God himself, then, who has "forever bent the back" of Israel in unbelief and caused them to "stumble".

Is it God's plan then, that the "hardened others" in Israel (11 : 7) have "stumbled" so as to finally and definitively "fall" into the hopelessness of unbelief (11 : 11 a)? "By no means!," Paul insists. On the contrary, it is through their "fall" (unbelief) that "salvation" has come to the Gentiles, so as to make Israel "jealous" (11 : 11 b; see 10 : 19). Unbelief is not God's final purpose for Israel. Rather, in God's salvific plan Israel's unbelief has been instrumental in bringing the Gentiles to faith and thus to hope for salvation. And the Gentiles' coming to faith through the unbelief of Israel likewise plays a part in God's future plan to finally bring unbelieving Israel to faith by making them "jealous" of the Gentiles. God's final purpose for Israel, then, is not a definitive "fall" into unbelief (11 : 11 a), but their future coming to faith through "jealousy" of the Gentiles (11 : 11 b; 10 : 19). Within God's salvific plan there is still hope that unbelieving Israel will come to faith, a hope that is interrelated to the faith and hope of the Gentiles.

Paul begins to explain this interrelation by revealing how important Israel's future coming to faith is for the hope of Christians. If the "full number" of Israel comes to faith, then the future eschatological salvation for which Christians hope will be that much greater. As Paul reasons, "if their (Israel's) fall (unbelief) means wealth (God's salvation, see 11 : 11 b) for the world and their deficiency (in coming to faith) means wealth for the Gentiles, how much more their full number (11 : 12)!" The future, final salvation, the "wealth," that will follow upon the full number of Israel coming to faith means a future goal of hope which will far surpass the "wealth" that has followed upon the failure of Israel as a whole to believe.

Paul then turns to the Gentiles (11 : 13 a) and informs them of his own special, apostolic hope (see 1 : 1-14) of arousing Israel to faith. As an "apostle to the Gentiles" Paul purposefully magnifies his ministry to them (11 : 13 b) "in the hope that perhaps, somehow I might make my flesh (Israel) jealous" (of the faith of the Gentiles) and "save" some of the Israelites by bringing them to faith (11 : 14). It is part of Paul's hope as an apostle, then, that his ministry of leading Gentiles to obedient faith (see 1 : 5) will be incorporated into God's overall salvific plan of eventually leading Israel as a whole to faith (see 10 : 19; 11 : 11). Paul informs the Gentiles that his apostolic ministry to them has an interrelation and ulterior motive with regard to Israel's future coming to faith. There is an interrelation because not only will the coming to faith of Gentiles benefit unbelieving

Israel by making them "jealous," but conversely, the future coming to faith of Israel will benefit Gentiles by bringing about an even greater future goal of hope for all. For if Israel's "rejection" (by God, in their not yet coming to faith) means "reconciliation" (with God) for the world, what will their "acceptance" (by God, in their coming to faith) mean but "life from the dead" (11 : 15)? Israel's future, then, remains most important for the hope of Paul, Gentiles and all Christians. Israel's future coming to faith will mean a much greater future goal of hope for the Gentiles and the whole world—God's future, final "life from the dead."

Having broadened the goal of Christian hope by adding to it the hope for Israel's future coming to faith, Paul reminds Gentiles that their hope ultimately rests upon the holy origins of Israel. The hope for Israel's future coming to faith is based upon Israel's "holy first-fruits" and "holy root": "If the (dough offered as) first-fruit is holy (see Num 15 : 17-21), so is the mass (of dough); and if the root is holy, so are the branches" (11 : 16). There is still hope that God will bring the holy "branches," individual Israelites, to faith because of their "holy root," the patriarchs (see 11 : 28).[28] Paul advises the Gentiles not to, "boast against" the "branches" of the olive tree which is Israel (see Jer 11 : 26), just because some of the branches, unbelieving Israelites, have been "broken off": For "you," the Gentile who are a wild olive shoot, have been grafted in among them (believing Israelites) and have become a sharer in the rich root of the olive tree (11 : 17). And if the Gentile should "boast against" the Israelite "branches," Paul reminds him that "you do not support the root but the root (supports) you" (11 : 18). It would thus be an arrogant presumption for the Gentiles to "boast against"[29] or vaunt themselves over the Israelites, for then they would be failing to realize that their Christian hope has its true and firm foundation in the same "holy" and "rich root" which they share with the Israelite "branches". In other words, the Christian hope of which Gentiles can "boast" (see 5 : 2 b.3.11) is "rooted" in Israel's holy origins (the patriarchs) so that there is no room for Gentiles "boasting against" Israelites.

Paul admits the truth of the Gentile's assertion that "branches (Israelites) were broken off (from the "root") in order that I (the Gentile) might be grafted in" (11 : 19). But he reminds the Gentile that his having been "grafted into" the holy root of Israel, and the future hope that goes with such a sharing of the "rich root" (patriarchal promises), is based solely on "faith": It is only because of their "unbelief" that Israelites have been broken off from the root, and it is only because of their "faith" that Gentiles remain grafted into the root (11 : 20 a). Therefore, Gentiles should not beco-

---

[28] Schlier, *Römerbrief,* 332; Wilckens, *Römer,* 2. 246; Michel, *Römer,* 348.

[29] "Boasting," as we have seen, expresses hope in Romans: 2 : 17.23; 3 : 27; 4 : 2; 5 : 2.3.11; 15 : 17.

me arrogantly "proud" but should rather "fear" God in reverent awe and humility (11 : 20 b). For if God did not spare the natural branches who did not believe, then he will certainly not spare "you," the Gentile, if you do not continue to believe (11 : 21). Because it so much depends upon continuing in faith, then, Christian hope includes a reverent fear and awesome humility before God.

Then Paul shows how radically dependent Christian hope is upon God. Hope is based upon faith, but it is ultimately God himself who initiates and continues our standing in faith. Paul reminds the Gentile of the "kindness" and "severity" of God—his "severity" is evident upon those who have "fallen" because he has not yet brought them to faith, and his "kindness" is evident upon "you," the Gentile, whom he has brought to faith, but provided that "you" remain in his kindness by continuing to believe, otherwise "you" also will be "cut off" from the root, your basis of hope (11 : 22). And conversely, if God allows individual Israelites not to remain in their unbelief but to finally come to faith, then there is hope that they "will be grafted" back into the holy root (11 : 23 a). And this hope for Israelites that Paul now arouses is based upon the "power" of God to bring them to faith, for "God has the power to graft them in again" (11 : 23 b). Paul strengthens this hope for Israelites by interrelating it to God's power with regard to the Gentiles. For if God manifested his salvific "power" in cutting "you," the Gentile, from what is by nature a wild olive tree, and grafting you against nature into a cultivated olive tree (Israel), then how much more certainly will God show his salvific "power" in grafting the natural branches (Israelites) back into *their own* olive tree (11 : 24)! The hope that Israelites "*will be grafted*" back into their own olive tree by coming to faith is based upon the salvific "power" of God, a power which he has already manifested in "grafting" in the Gentiles by bringing them to faith. If God brought Gentiles to faith, then the hope is certain that he can and will bring Israelites to faith.

We have seen that in God's salvific plan the hope of Christians is interrelated to the situation of Israel in the following ways: 1) The unbelief of Israel has meant that hope for "salvation" was given to the Gentiles to make Israel "jealous," so that Israel's future coming to faith will give Christians an even greater future goal of hope (11 : 11-15). 2) The hope of Paul's apostolate to the Gentiles is interrelated to Israel's future coming to faith; by leading Gentiles to faith Paul hopes to make Israel "jealous" and thus save some of them; this will mean a greater hope for all Christians (11 : 13-15). 3) Christian hope has its foundation in Israel's own holy origins (patriarchal promises), so that "boasting against" Israelites would be a vain presumption (11 : 16-18). 4) Just as Christians have hope only if they believe, so Israelites will have hope if only they believe. And one's coming to and remaining in faith depends ultimately upon God, so that Christian hope includes a reverent and humble "fear" of God (11 : 19-21). 5) The hope that God can and will bring individual Israelites to faith is all the more certain because he has already brought Gentiles to a faith and hope which is based upon Israel's own holy and rich "root" (11 : 17-18.22-24).

E. **Paul Proclaims the Hope That "All Israel Will Be Saved!»: Rom 11 : 25-36**

Paul climactically culminates his previously expressed hope for Israel by revealing a "mystery" of God's salvific plan, namely, that "a hardening has come upon part of Israel until the full number of Gentiles come in, and thus all Israel will be saved!" (11 : 25 b-26 a). This "mystery" explains God's way that "all Israel will be saved": the "hardening" (of unbelief) that has come upon part of Israel is temporary; it will remain only until it has completed its role within God's plan of bringing the full number (as determined by God) of Gentiles into the community of end-time salvation (see 11 : 11.17), and "thus," *in this way*, will all Israel be saved! In other words, if the present unbelief of "part" of Israel is only temporary and, moreover, if it serves God's salvific purpose of bringing the "full number" of Gentiles to faith, then this mysterious plan of God motivates Paul to the sure hope that "thus" *all* Israel will be saved! This broadened hope that "*all*" Israel "will be saved" thus develops the previous hope (9 : 27) that a "remnant" of Israel "will be saved." And Paul's hope that Israel as a whole, as God's specially chosen people, will be saved climaxes the previous hope (11 : 22-24) that God can and will bring individual Israelites to faith, so that Israel as a whole will no longer be an unbelieving, "disobedient and contrary people" (10 : 21).

Paul's hope that all Israel will be saved carries important consequences for the hope of all Christians. Paul explicitly addresses "this mystery" to his Christian "brethren" in Rome and underscores the importance of its communication to them by introducing it with the rhetorically emphatic formula, "I want you indeed to understand" (11 : 25 a).[30] He informs them of "this mystery" lest they become "wise in their own estimation" (11 : 25 a). Paul already warned Gentiles against "boasting over" Israel (11 : 18), an arrogant presumption because it fails to recognize that Christian hope for future "salvation" (11 : 11) and "life from the dead" (11 : 15) rests ultimately upon Israel's "holy root," the patriarchal promises. Paul also warned them against "thinking proud thoughts" (11 : 20 b) based on their present situation of faith (11 : 20 a); such a pride from one's faith would amount to a haughty overconfidence because it fails to realize that "faith" is not ultimately one's own doing but a gift from God. And now Paul warns his fellow Christians

---

[30] See Rom 1 : 13; 1 Cor 10 : 1; 12 : 1; 2 Cor 1 : 8; 1 Thes 4 : 13; Wilckens, *Römer,* 2. 252; Schlier, *Römerbrief,* 337-338.

against a hope which "relies on their own wisdom" (11 : 25 a) as he opens them to God's wisdom (see 11 : 33) with its broader hope that all Israel will be saved. A hope which is based upon their own way of thinking about Israel's future because of present unbelief would limit the future goal of Christian hope, but "this mystery" of God's plan broadens the future goal of our hope to include the salvation of *all* Israel.

With a combined quotation of Isa 59 : 20-21 a and 27 : 9, Paul undergirds the certainty of his hope that all Israel will be saved, for, as written, "out of Zion will come the Deliverer, he will turn away ungodliness from Jacob"; "and this will be my covenant for them, when I take away their sins" (11 : 26 b-27). This prophetic promise, whose future fulfillment is assured because it is the unfailing word of God (see 9 : 6 a), confirms the hope for the future salvation of all Israel in accord with "this mystery" (11 : 25 a) of God's salvific plan. The hoped-for salvation of all Israel, then, accords with and includes the sure hope that God will turn away their "ungodliness" and manifest his covenant fidelity on their behalf by forgiving their "sins". This hope thus implies that presently unbelieving Israel will be saved, like Christians, by finally believing in God's justification (through Christ's death) of their "ungodliness" and forgiveness of their sins (see esp. 4 : 5-8; also 3 : 23-26; 5 : 6-8).

Paul then even further bolsters his hope that all Israel will be saved: First, that Israelites are "enemies" (unbelievers, see 11 : 20 a.23 a) of God as regards the gospel plays a positive role within God's salvific plan since it is "for your (the Christian's) sake" (11 : 28 a), that is, for your belief in the gospel which brings your salvation (see 11 : 11). Secondly, as regards God's previous "election" the Israelites are still "beloved" by God "because of the patriarchs" (11 : 28 b; see 9 : 4-5.6 b-13). And thirdly, the "gifts" and the "call" that God has already bestowed upon Israel through the patriarchs (9 : 4-5.12-13) are "irrevocable" (11 : 29), and thus still serve as a foundation of hope for Israel. For these reasons, then, the hope that all Israel will be saved (11 : 26 a) is all the more certain.

The hope that *all* Israel will be saved within God's salvific plan acquires even greater assurance as Paul demonstrates how it is based upon the "mercy" that God has already given to "you" Christians precisely because of Israel's unbelief. And that God will ultimately show his "mercy" to all Israel just as he has already shown mercy to "you" Christians illustrates why Christians should not hold to a limited hope which relies on their own wisdom (11 : 25 a) but should broaden the future goal of their hope to include God's mercy (11 : 32) and salvation (11 : 26 a.11) for all—the Gentiles and Israel. For, according to God's plan, just as "you" Christians once were "disobedient" (in unbelief) to God, but now "have received mercy" because of Israel's "disobedience" (unbelief), so they have now been "disobedient" for the benefit of the "mercy" shown to you in order that they may now "receive mercy" (11 : 30-31). Because the respective salvation-historical roles of the Gentiles and Israel have been so inextricably interwoven by God, the hope is sure that just as God's mercy has already begun to overcome the disobedient unbelief of the Gentiles, so "now"[31] in the time open to the eschatological future which has already begun, God's mercy will certainly overcome the disobedient unbelief of Israel. Paul then sums up this broadened hope which we Christians may now have for "all" based on the mercy God has already shown them: For God has "imprisoned" all in the disobedience of first not believing in order that he may then "have mercy" on all (11 : 32) (Gentiles and Israel) by bringing them to faith (see 11 : 22-23) and salvation (11 : 11.26 a). Based on the limitless, universal mercy of God, authentic Christian hope can and must remain radically open to the future of God—the future manifestation of his mercy and salvation for all—including *all* Israel.

Paul concludes Rom 9 – 11 by exuberantly and eloquently praising the God of unlimited hope. In view of the humanly incomprehensible "mystery" of God's plan which arouses the hope that *all* Israel will be saved (11 : 26 a) and that God will have mercy on *all* (11 : 32 b), Paul can only stand in humble awe of the overwhelming and unfathomable depth of the "riches" and "wisdom" and "knowledge" of God (11 : 33 a). So "unsearchable" are God's decisions and so "inscrutable" his ways (11 : 33 b) within his universal plan of salvation, that Christian hope for the future cannot rely on merely human wisdom (11 : 25 a) but must remain totally open to the future of God. For about God's salvific plan the scriptures testify that there is no human being who can fully know the mind of God, no one who can become his adviser (Isa 40 : 13), and no one who can place God in his debt (Job 35 : 7; 41 : 11) (11 : 34-35). Hence, there is no human being who can calculate or control, comprehend or fully grasp, the unfathomable riches, wisdom and knowledge of God (11 : 33 a). Therefore, our Christian hope based on this unlimited greatness of God and his plan for universal salvation can and must remain open to God's incalculable and uncontrollable future. God's power and will to save far exceeds what human beings can think or imagine. Christian hope looks to the humanly unfathomable future salvation of God, because "all things" not only came "from" and "through" God but have their future, final goal "in" God (11 : 36 a). It is God who holds ultimate power and control over all things, so that the incalculably great God stands as the basis, the means and the future goal of our Christian hope for the merciful salvation of all—"to him be glory forever! Amen!" (11 : 36 b).

With regard to our theme of hope, then, we have seen that 1) Paul has enlarged the future goal of hope to include the hope that *all* Israel will be saved (11 : 25-27). 2) This hope for Israel is based on the "mercy" God has

---

[31] For the reasons to retain *nyn*, "now," in 11 : 31 b, see Metzger, *A Textual Commentary*, 527.

already shown previously "disobedient" Christians, so that now there is hope that God will have mercy on *all*—Gentiles and Israel (11 : 28-32).   3) The broadened hope for *all* Israel means that Christian hope should not be limited by mere human wisdom (11 : 25 a) but can and must rely upon the unfathomable wealth, wisdom and knowledge of God for a hope open to the incalculable and unlimited future salvation of God (11 : 33-36).

F. Summary

We may summarize the results of our examination of hope in Rom 9 – 11 as follows: 1) God's word (9 : 6 a) remains a valid foundation of Christian hope despite Israel's failure to believe (9 : 22-26), and the enduring word and salvific purpose of God still supports hope for unbelieving Israel as well (9 : 6a.11 b.27-29). Christian hope for salvation rests firmly upon Israel's own holy origins, God's word of promise to the patriarchs (11 : 16-18). And the hope that all Israel will be saved within God's salvific plan stems from the mercy God has already shown previously disobedient Christians (11 : 26 a.28-32).

2) Despite every opportunity provided by God Israel as a people has failed to believe in the gospel (9 : 30-10 : 21). But faith is still available to Israel. For Christian hope depends solely on faith, so that just as Christians have hope only if they believe, so Israelites will have hope if only they believe (11 : 19-21).

3) Since coming to and remaining in faith depends ultimately upon God's free gift, the attitude of Christian hope includes a reverent and humble "fear" of God (11 : 19-21). Christian hope excludes "boasting over" Israel (11 : 18), becoming proud of one's own status in faith (11 : 20), and being wise in one's own estimation about the future of God (11 : 25 a). On the other hand, Christian hope implies an awe and joyful praise in view of the unlimited future salvation which is based on the unfathomable depth of God's wealth, wisdom and knowledge (11 : 33-36).

4) Hope must always remain open to the future of the sovereign God who freely calls (9 : 12 a) and shows his mercy (9 : 16.23-26). Israel's future coming to faith through jealousy of the Gentiles means an even greater future goal for Christian hope (11 : 11-15). In accord with the secret mystery of God's salvific plan the future goal of Christian hope must be broad enough to include the hope that all Israel will be saved (11 : 25-27). Since we Christians may now hope that God will show his mercy to "all" (11 : 28-32), our hope can and must be radically open to the incalculable, uncontrollable and limitless future salvation of God (11 : 33-36).

In reaching the climactic hope that all Israel will be saved Paul has continued his purpose of arousing and strengthening the hope of his fellow

Christians (1 : 11-12). The hope that he proclaims in Rom 9 – 11, then, develops and complements the hope he expresses in Rom 1 – 8 in the following ways: 1) The reliable foundation of Christian hope in the love of God for us in the death-resurrection of Christ and gift of the Spirit (5 : 5-8; 8 : 9-11.23.26-27) gains strength because God's word (9 : 6 a) and salvific purpose (9 : 11 b) endures for Christians despite Israel's failure to believe. The basis of Christian hope is broadened to include Israel's holy origins (11 : 16-18). And moreover, the same mercy and love which God has already given Christians (9 : 23-24; 11 : 17.22.28-32) stimulates the hope that all Israel will be saved (11 : 26 a).

2) As in Rom 1 – 8 (see 1 : 16; 3 : 21-26; 4 : 1-25; 5 : 1-11) so in Rom 9 – 11 (see 9 : 30 – 10 : 13), Christian hope still depends upon faith, even though Israel does not yet believe (10 : 19-21). Faith is still available to "all," then, and "all" who do believe have hope for the future, final salvation of God (10 : 6-13). But faith always remains the free gift of the sovereign God (11 : 19-21).

3) Rom 1 – 8 emphasized the confident, eager expectation, steadfastness and joyful "boasting" aspects of hope because of the certainty of our future hope despite present difficulties (1 : 16; 4 : 18-21; 5 : 1-11; 8 : 18-39). Rom 9 – 11 complements this by emphasizing the humble, reverent and awe-inspiring aspects of hope because of its total openness to God's future salvation which exceeds all human calculation and comprehension (11 : 18-21.25 a.33-36).

4) In Rom 1 – 8 the future goal of Christian hope, God's glory and salvation, is so great that it will far surpass present sufferings (5 : 2-5; 8 : 18-30); and the attainment of this goal is absolutely assured by God himself, so that "we will certainly be saved" (5 : 9-10) as nothing "will ever be able to separate us from the love of God in Christ" (8 : 31-39). Rom 9 – 11 complements this by broadening the future goal of Christian hope to include the hope that *all* Israel will be saved (11 : 26 a). Israel's future salvation will mean an even greater future goal of hope for all (11 : 11-15). This broadened future goal of hope is assured in accord with God's salvific purpose, as God will finally have mercy on *all* (11 : 32). In Rom 9 – 11, then, the future goal of Christian hope goes beyond the limits of human understanding; it is the future *of God*—a future of unlimited and total salvation which exceeds human expectation and imagination, for "*all things* are from him and through him and to him; glory be to him forever! Amen!" (11 : 33-36).

Chapter VI

Hope and Christian Living: Rom 12 : 1 – 15 : 13

Paul now exhorts, encourages and directs his fellow Christians to the way of communal living and everyday practical conduct that follows as a natural consequence of the gospel of hope. This exhortation or parenesis, however, is not simply an added appendix but an integral part of the proclamation of the gospel, as it extends and applies the reality of God's justification by faith and consequent hope to the concrete realm of Christian living. Paul develops this parenetic section as follows: A) With exhortations of a more general and fundamental character he indicates how Christians live now in accord with their hope (12 : 1 – 13 : 14). B) And with regard to a specific rift within the Roman community, he demonstrates how the "strong" and the "weak" must exercise love in order to maintain hope (14 : 1 – 15 : 13).

A. Christians Live Now in Accord with Their Hope: Rom 12 : 1 – 13 : 14

In this first main subdivision Paul proceeds thus: He initiates his parenesis with a general and fundamental exhortation for Christians to live now in accord with the hope Paul has previously proclaimed (12 : 1-2), and this serves as the thematic heading for the entire section; he then begins to concretely illustrate how Christians are to live in accord with their hope (12 : 3-8)—he exhorts them to the proper functioning of the various charisms that God has granted specific individuals for the benefit of the Christian community; he voices numerous exhortations revolving around the theme of the genuine *agapē* or "love" which Christians are to exercise toward others (12 : 9-21); he directs Christians to be submissive to the ruling political authorities (13 : 1-7); he reverts to the exhortation to love one another as the fulfillment of God's Law (13 : 8-10); and he concludes with general exhortations which give an eschatological urgency to his parenesis, as he reminds his fellow Christians of the nearness of our future salvation, the goal of our hope (13 : 11-14).

1. *We should submit ourselves to serve the God of hope: Rom 12 : 1-2*

Paul opens with a basic exhortation that establishes the context and sets the tone for his subsequent exhortations. As a consequence of all that he has previously proclaimed, Paul encouragingly exhorts his fellow Christians "by the mercies of God to offer your bodies as a living sacrifice, holy and pleasing to God, which is your spiritual worship" (12 : 1). That God has now graciously justified sinners through his merciful forgiveness (1 : 16-17; 3 : 21 – 4 : 25), has displayed his compassionate love for us as sinners (5 : 1-11; 8 : 31-39); and that God "will have mercy" on all (11 : 32), including all Israel (11 : 26 a), as he has already bestowed his mercy on Christians (9 : 15.23-25; 11 : 30-32) stimulates Paul and his fellow Christians to hope for the future glory and salvation of God (5 : 1-11; 8 : 18-39; 10 : 9-13; 11 : 11.26 a). These are the "mercies of God" which form the basis of the hope proclaimed in Rom 1 – 11 and now give rise to Paul's encouraging exhortation. Paul now exhorts us Christians to live our new life of hope as he has previously described it. He has already exhorted us to live our new future hope now by living in dedication to the God of hope: He encouraged us to consider ourselves already "dead" to the death-bringing hopelessness of sin, but "living" to God, the goal of our hope (6 : 11). We can and must "offer" ourselves "to God" as those who have been brought from the hopelessness of being "dead" to the hope of "living" (6 : 13). And we must now "offer" our members as slaves to God's righteousness which leads to our "holiness," God's sanctification, the future goal of our hope (6 : 19). Similarly, Paul now exhorts us Christians to "offer" our bodies as a "living" sacrifice, "holy" and pleasing "to God". The hope based on the "mercies of God" has freed us from the hopelessness of sin and death so that we may now "live" in hope for God. And whereas in our former hopelessness we could not "please" God (8 : 8), we may now offer ourselves as a "pleasing" sacrifice to God (12 : 1 b).

Paul continues by urging us not to be "conformed to this present age" (12 : 2 a). We Christians are to live out our future hope now by continually[1] and critically distancing ourselves from "this present age," the hopeless age which is under the powers of sin and death. We must, then, already be conformed to "the age to come," God's future age, the goal of our hope. But how can we already live our hope in this present age of hopelessness? Paul's answer: "be continually transformed in the renewal of your mind, so that you may determine what is the will of God, what is good and pleasing

---

[1] The present imperative in 12 : 2 has iterative significance; Wilckens, *Römer*, 3. 7.

and perfect" (12 : 2 b). Paul previously explained how we baptized Christians can already live the future "life" for which we hope by "walking," that is, conducting ourselves or living, in "newness of life" (6 : 4). We have been freed from our old captivity to hopelessness under the Law, so that we can now live out our future hope by serving God in the "newness of the Spirit" (7 : 6).[2] And similarly, the "renewal of the mind" or the renewed way of thinking that comes with our new hope must be allowed to continually transform our present lives, so that they conform not to "this present age" but to our future hope. This renewed way of thinking enables us to "determine" or "decide" what is the "will of God" in our everyday living. In other words, we now can and must do what is "good" and "pleasing" and "perfect" in our everyday Christian conduct. In our former hopelessness to the indwelling power of sin under the Law (7 : 7-25) it was impossible to do what was "good" (7 : 18-20), the "good" commandment or will of God (7 : 12). But we are now enabled by God's renewal of our mind to do "the good," the "will of God," in our everyday living and thereby conform our lives to the future, final "good" for which we hope (see 8 : 28; 10 : 15). By doing "the good" now we promote and maintain our hope for God's future salvation.

2. We should use our charisms to promote hope: Rom 12 : 3-8

Paul applies his fundamental exhortation to live hope now by a renewed way of thinking to the proper functioning of the various charisms within the Christian community at Rome. Through the special apostolic grace God gave him (12 : 3 a; 1 : 5) Paul exhorts each and every member of the community about the use of the charisms God has given them (12 : 6-8). No one should "overstrive" in the exercise of a particular charism beyond what "is necessary," that is, beyond God's will for the good of the community (12 : 3 b). Such an "overstriving" would neither promote nor maintain future hope because it fails to accord with the good will of God (12 : 2). One should rather "strive" so as to "strive prudently" in the use of his charism (12 : 3 c), in accord with the measure of faith God has apportioned to each (12 : 3 d). In that way the various charisms will function properly for the good of the many members who are one body in Christ (12 : 4-5). In other words, the different charisms among the many members should be exercised with a care and concern, a "love" (12 : 9 a), for each and every member, who is an important and integral part of the one body of Christ. Thus the

---

[2] For similar Pauline expressions of "newness" or "renewal" in Christian life, see 2 Cor 4 : 16; 5 : 17; Gal 6 : 15.

"good," the will of God, will be accomplished for the community so as to preserve and promote hope for the future.

3. *We should love one another in, through and for hope: Rom 12 : 9-21*

All of Paul's directives center upon "love," the fraternal care and concern that all Christians are to actively manifest toward others. The "genuine love" (12 : 9 a) that is part of our spiritual worship (12 : 1) now possible because of God's renewal of our thinking (12 : 2)[3] preserves our hope for God's future "good," since it includes "abhorring[4] the evil and clinging to the good" (12 : 9 b), God's "good" will for our everyday living (12 : 2).

The warm, brotherly love and respect we are to show one another (12 : 10) is to be performed in and through our new attitude of hope. The Spirit, as the basis of our hope (see 5 : 5; 8 : 1-27), incites us to a burning zeal (12 : 11 b) with which we are to persevere (12 : 11 a) in loving one another, and thereby serve the Lord (12 : 11 c).[5] In loving one another we are to "rejoice *in hope*" (*tę elpidi chairontes*, 12 : 12 a). Genuine Christian love, then, is to be accompanied by the joy that comes from our confident hope for God's future salvation; it is to be performed in joyful hope. Hope also enables us to persevere in loving one another. Distress or suffering need not interrupt, prevent or destroy love, for it is part of Christian hope to "be steadfast in suffering" (12 : 12 b) (see 5 : 3-4; 8 : 18-25.35-37). And the continual praying which is part of hope's perseverance also enables Christians to persevere in genuine love, as Paul exhorts us to "remain constant in prayer" (12 : 12 c). Since in prayer we express our hope for the future completion of God's salvific will (see 8 : 26-27), being constant in prayer, by keeping us aware of our future hope, enables us to continue our genuine love for

---

[3] On *agapē* in Rom 12 : 9 Cranfield (*Romans*, 630) explains:

> ... God in His love has claimed us wholly for Himself and for our neighbours, and the love, of which Paul speaks here, is the believer's 'yes', in thought and feeling, word and deed, unconditional and without reservation, to that total claim of the loving God, in so far as it relates to the neighbour—a 'yes', which is no human possibility but the gracious work of the Holy Spirit.

[4] On the imperatival force of the following participles, adjectives and infinitives in 12 : 9-19, see Zerwick, *Biblical Greek*, § 373; A. P. Salom, "The Imperatival Use of the Participle in the NT," *AusBR* 11 (1963) 41-49.

[5] On the text-critical problem in 12 : 11 c and the choice for this reading, see Metzger, *A Textual Commentary*, 528; Schlier, *Römerbrief*, 376-377; Cranfield, *Romans*, 634-636.

one another. We are to love one another, then, in and through the joy, steadfastness and prayer that are essential to our hope for the future of God.

In and through such hope Christians are to show genuine love by "contributing to the needs of the saints" and "practising hospitality" (12 : 13).
Confident hope for God's future salvation (12 : 12 a) enables us not only to
remain steadfast in suffering (12 : 12 b) but even to invoke God's salvific
blessing rather than a curse upon our persecutors (12 : 14). Our joyful hope
(12 : 12 a) enables us to love one another by not only sharing in the joy but
also in the sorrow of others (12 : 15). The humility and openness to God's
future which is part of authentic hope (see 11 : 20.25) forbids us from a
proud, individualistic thinking or striving which could divide the community,
and bids us instead to associate with the lowly so as to show the same genuine love to all (12 : 16).

Finally, Paul exhorts Christians to make every effort to live in harmon-
ious peace and love with all for the sake of their future hope in God. We
should never repay evil with evil, but should rather have a regard for what is
good before all (12 . 17). As far as possible, we should take it upon ourselves
to promote peace with all (12 : 18). Because of our hope for God's future
salvation for all, we should never avenge ourselves, but should rather leave
vindication to God's future wrath, in accord with God's scriptural promise
(Deut 32 : 35): "Vindication is mine, I will repay, says the Lord" (12 : 19).
And in accord with Prov 25 : 21-22 we should care for the needs of our enemies because of the possibility of contributing to their conversion: "If your
enemy is hungry, feed him; if he is thirsty, give him drink; for by so doing
you will heap burning coals upon his head" (12 : 20).[6] We must "not be
conquered by the evil, but rather conquer the evil with the good" (12 : 21).
We Christians, then, are to do the "good," the will of God for the here and
now (12 : 1), by showing genuine love (12 : 9 a) toward all, even toward enemies, and thereby keep our hope authentically open to the future of God.
In, through and for the sake of our hope we are to have a genuine love for
all (12 : 9-21).

4. We should submit to governing authorities for the sake of hope: Rom 13 : 1-7

In the light of all that we have seen about the importance of hope for
Christian life and faith, we can say that submitting to the governing authorities promotes and maintains Christian hope because it is the same as submitting to God (13 : 1), the basis and ultimate goal of hope. Those who would

---

[6] For suggestions of more precise interpretations of Rom 12 : 20 b (Prov 25 : 22),
see Schlier, *Römerbrief*, 383; Wilckens, *Römer*, 3. 26; Michel, *Römer*, 392.

resist these authorities would be resisting the order established by God (13 : 2 a), and would therefore pervert their hope for God's future salvation into despair, as "they will receive condemnation" (13 : 2 b). All must submit to God-established authority in order to live in accord with hope for future salvation and thereby avoid God's future condemnation. Authority, God's servant for the "good" (13 : 4), helps us to live out our hope for God's future "good" (see 8 : 28) here and now as it provokes us to do the "good" (13 : 4.5), God's will for everyday living (12 : 2). Doing God's "good" now promotes and maintains our hope for God's future "good" rather than his future "wrath" (13 : 4). Therefore, all are to submit to the authorities by paying the debts, taxes, revenue, respect and honor due them (13 : 6-7) not only for the sake of our hope to avoid God's "wrath," but also for the sake of our "conscience" (13 : 5; see 2 : 15) by which, with our renewed way of thinking (12 : 2), we can live out future hope now.

5. *We should love one another to fulfill God's Law and thus promote hope: Rom 13 : 8-10*

Here Paul climaxes his preceding exhortations regarding Christian love. The only obligation we should "owe" (see 13 : 7 a) others is love, for the one who loves the other has fulfilled God's Law (13 : 8.10 b). Such summary commandments of the Law as "You shall not commit adultery, you shall not kill, you shall not steal, you shall not covet" (Exod 20 : 13-15 = Deut 5 : 17-19.21), and any other commandment, are summed up by Lev 19 : 18 b, "You shall love your neighbor as yourself" (13 : 9).[7] Love does no "evil" to the neighbor (13 : 10 a), it rather effects the "good" (12 : 2.9.17; 13 : 3-4) that Paul has been exhorting as the way to live out Christian hope.

6. *We should live according to hope now because our future hope is always coming closer: Rom 13 : 11-14.*

The future hope that comes nearer to us every day serves as the decisively urgent motivation to live now in a way that corresponds with our new hope. Paul's preceding exhortations centering on "love" and the "good" (12 : 1 – 13 : 10) are all the more serious and urgent now that God's future "salvation," the goal of our hope,[8] is closer to us than when we first came to

---

[7] See Gal 5 : 14; Matt 5 : 43; 19 : 18-19; Mark 12 : 31; Luke 10 : 27; Jas 2 : 8.
[8] See 1 : 16; 5 : 9.10; 8 : 24; 9 : 27; 10 : 1.9.10.13; 11 : 11.26.

believe (13 : 11). As the "night" is already far advanced and the "day" is at hand (13 : 12 a), our future hope is constantly coming closer to us. It is most urgent, then, that we not conform to "this present age" (12 : 2) of hopelessness but cast off the works of darkness and put on the armor of light (13 : 12 b). Since we are now in the "daylight" of our new hope, we should "walk," that is, conduct ourselves properly (13 : 13 a)—in accord with our renewed way of thinking in our present situation of hope (12 : 2). Such conduct excludes reveling and drunkenness, sexual excess and debauchery (hopeless conduct of the darkness of the night), rivalry and jealousy (conduct against communal Christian love) (13 : 13 b). By the renewal of our mind (12 : 2), then, we must entertain no forethought of the flesh to satisfy its desires (13 : 14 b) and thereby slide back into the dark night of hopelessness (see 6 : 12; 7 : 7-25). Rather, in accord with the hope that comes from our baptismal faith (see 6 : 1-11) we are to "clothe ourselves" with the Lord Jesus Christ (13 : 14 a). It is urgently necessary, then, that we live out our new hope now by conduct in accord with our future, ever closer "salvation".

B. The "Strong" and the "Weak" Must Show Love to Maintain Hope: Rom 14 : 1 – 15 : 13

The second main subdivision of Paul's parenesis (14 : 1 – 15 : 13) concerns the Christian love and peace that should prevail between two groups within the Roman community, the so-called "strong" and the "weak" in faith.[9] Paul does not fully disclose the precise details involved in this rift. The "weak," however, are those who believe that they should not eat meat, which they consider to be "unclean" (14 : 2.14), nor drink wine (14 : 21), and who observe special days (14 : 5-6). The "strong," on the other hand, among whom Paul includes himself (14 : 14; 15 : 1) are convinced that they may eat meat and drink wine since these things are not "unclean" in themselves (14 : 2.14.20-21), and they do not "esteem one day over another" (14 : 5-6). Even here, hope plays a role in the way Paul tackles this problem: 1) He first exhorts them against judging one another now in view of hope (14 : 1-12). 2) He then admonishes them against conduct which would destroy the hope of others (14 : 13-23). Then he calls upon us Christians to maintain hope by steadfastness and encouragement (15 : 1-6). 4) Paul finally invites us all to love one another so that our hope may increase and abound (15 : 7-13).

---

[9] For a full discussion of Rom 14 : 1-23, including attempts to elucidate the rift between the "strong" and the "weak," see Schlier, *Römerbrief,* 400-418; Michel, *Römer,* 418-441; Wilckens, *Römer,* 3. 79-97, 109-115; Cranfield, *Romans,* 690-729; Käsemann, *Romans,* 364-380.

1. *Do not judge one another in view of your future hope: Rom 14 : 1-12*

Paul exhorts those who consider themselves "strong" to "welcome" those considered "weak" in faith (14 : 1). This welcoming (see also 14 : 2; 15 : 1.7) exemplifies Christian love (see 14 : 15) by the fraternal respect and concern these Christians are to have for one another despite the differences in their convictions. They should not "judge" nor "despise" one another (14 : 3.10.13), since both groups belong to and serve the same Lord with their different convictions (14 : 4-6). No one lives or dies for himself (14 : 7) but for the same Lord of us all (14 : 8; see 6 : 8-11). For Christ died and came to life precisely that he might rule over all of us, not only when we are dead but while we are living (14 : 9). Once we die we will all stand before the judgment seat of God (14 : 10). *God* himself and no other will judge us all, for as God promises in the scriptures: "As *I* live, says the Lord (Isa 49 : 18), every knee shall bow to *me*, and every tongue shall praise *God*" (Isa 45 : 23) (14 : 11). Each of us must give account of himself to God (14 : 12). Thus, we should live in accord with our hope by leaving judgment entirely to the future of God; we should not judge one another now for the sake of our future hope of *God's* judgment of all. Once again, future hope motivates present Christian love.

2. *Do not let your conduct destroy the hope of others: Rom 14 : 13-23*

Not only should we no longer judge one another, but we should take care not to place an obstacle before a fellow Christian (14 : 13). Paul himself is convinced in the Lord Jesus that nothing is "unclean" in itself, but becomes unclean for anyone who thinks it unclean (14 : 14). And those who are convinced that nothing is unclean must respect this. If one Christian is grieved because of what another eats, love is not prevailing in the community (14 : 15 a). And if love is not prevailing between the "strong" and the "weak," then they are not living in accord with Christian hope; they are not maintaining and promoting their future hope. Since Christ died for us so that we now have a sure hope for God's salvation (5 : 1-11; 8 : 31-39), we must cease from "destroying" with our food a fellow Christian for whom Christ has died (14 : 15 b). In other words, the "strong" must take care that their conduct of eating food does not destroy another's hope for salvation based on the death of Christ. We should not allow the "good" that we do as a Christian community by loving one another in accord with our hope[10] to be "defamed" or "blasphemed" by others (14 : 16). For the kingdom of God is not food and drink, but God's "righteousness" and "peace" and "joy" in the Holy Spirit (14 : 17)—future goals of hope already present through the gift of the Spirit. Thus, in this matter of "food" and "drink," the one who serves Christ in accord with righteousness, peace and joy in the Holy Spirit lives the new life of hope as one "pleasing" (see 12 : 1-2) to God and approved (rather than "defamed," see 14 : 16) by others (14 : 18). Therefore, as Paul sums up, let us live in accord with the kingdom of God for which we hope by pursuing what makes for peace and mutual edification (14 : 19).

Paul insists that we must not destroy the "work of God," the peace of the community through mutual edification, for the sake of food (14 : 20 a). Although everything is "clean," it is bad for the "weak" to eat what he considers "unclean" because of scandal given by the "strong" (14 : 20 b). The "strong" should keep the freedom their faith gives them between themselves and God (14 : 22) so as not to scandalize their "weak" brothers (14 : 21). In this way the "strong" will not destroy the "conviction" of the "weak". For if the "weak" eats in "doubt" he thereby loses his conviction as well as his future hope for salvation, since he then stands already "condemned" (14 : 23 a). Such a doubtful eating, because not done from faith, would result in the hopelessness of "sin" (14 : 23 b). Thus, Christians must not destroy another's hope by their own conduct, even when that conduct proceeds from their own strong conviction. Rather, they should love one another and thereby maintain and promote the hope of all.

3. *Through steadfastness and encouragement we maintain our hope: Rom 15 : 1-6*

Paul advises the "strong," among whom he includes himself, that they ought to "bear" the "weaknesses of the weak" (15 : 1 a). The "strong," precisely insofar as they are the stronger members of the community, have this obligation toward the "weak" as part of the general obligation of Christian love.[11] The "strong" ought to actively "endure" or "bear" (not simply "tolerate"!) the "weaknesses" of their weaker brothers as a manifestation of

---

[10] See 12 : 2.9.17.21; 13 : 3-4.10; Schlier, *Römerbrief*, 414-415; the change to the plural "your" (*hymōn*, see Metzger, *A Textual Commentary*, 532) indicates that 14 : 16 is addressed to the whole community (see the singular "you" (*sou*) in 14 : 15.21-22).

[11] Note Rom 13 : 8 a: "Owe no one anything, except to love one another..."; see also Rom 8 : 12 and Michel, *Römer*, 442.

Christian love.[12] In other words, the "strong" ought not to "please" themselves (15 : 1 b). From the context (14 : 1-23) this means that the "strong" ought not to eat the meat which the "weak" are convinced is "unclean". Such conduct would not be in accord with Christian love (14 : 15).

Paul extends his exhortation involving "pleasing" to each and every member of the community (15 : 2). "Each of us," the "strong" and the "weak" alike, must exercise love by pleasing his neighbor, and thus bring about the "good," the salvific will of God which furthers the hope of the community (12 : 2.9.17.21; 13 : 3-4.10; 14 : 16). Everyone "pleasing" and thus loving his neighbor results in the mutual "edification" of the community, part of our new situation of hope (see 14 : 16-19).[13]

That Christ "did not please himself" (15 : 3 a) should motivate the "strong" not to please themselves (15 : 1 b) and each member of the community to please his neighbor (15 : 2 a). Paul illustrates that Christ did not please himself by citing Ps 69 : 10 b: "The reproaches of those who reproached you fell upon me" (15 : 3 b). These words are to be understood as spoken by Christ in the context of his passion and death, so that the "reproaches" are those of men against God, which have fallen upon Christ.[14] Thus, in exhorting Christians to love by "pleasing" the other, Paul appeals to the love of Christ for us as manifested by his passion and death in accord with the scriptural plan of God (15 : 3).

Paul draws out the significance not only of the previous scriptural quotation but of all of the scriptures: "For whatever was written beforehand was written for our instruction" (15 : 4 a). Thus, the scriptures have relevance for our present age of hope in terms of the instruction they offer us for the daily situations of Christian living.[15]

Paul then arrives at the goal of his previous exhortation to love (15 : 1-2) and of the "instruction" offered by the scriptures (15 : 3): "that by steadfastness and by the encouragement of the scriptures we might have hope (*elpida*)." "Steadfastness" or persevering "endurance" (*hypomonē*) describes the attitude of Christ in not pleasing himself but rather taking upon himself the reproaches directed against God (15 : 3). Such "steadfastness" is necessary for the "strong" not to please themselves but to bear the weaknesses of the weak (15 : 1), and for all Christians to please their neighbor for the good of the community (15 : 2). Hence, "steadfastness" is essential to the exercise of

---

[12] F. Büchsel, "*bastazō*," *TDNT* 1 (1964) 596; BAGD, 137; Schlier, *Römerbrief*, 419; Michel, *Römer*, 443.

[13] On love "edifying" the Christian community elsewhere in Paul, see 1 Cor 8 : 1. And for ideas similar to that of Rom 15 : 2, see 1 Cor 10 : 23-24; 10 : 33-11 : 1.

[14] Schlier, *Römerbrief*, 420; Cranfield, *Romans*, 733-734; Michel, *Römer*, 444-445.

[15] See 4 : 22-24; 1 Cor 9 : 10; 10 : 11.

Christian love. As we have already seen, *hypomonē* is an attribute of hope in Romans (5 : 3-4; 8 : 25; 12 : 12), referring to an active steadfastness or persevering endurance in the face of suffering as one awaits the future completion of God's salvific will. In the midst of suffering, hope takes the form of "steadfastness," which, in turn produces new hope (see 5 : 3-4). And it is "by steadfastness" that we "have," that is, "maintain" or "keep," hope (*tēn elpida echomen*) (15 : 4).[16] Here the relationship between Christian love and hope becomes more explicit. The point of intersection between hope and love resides in "steadfastness," which is essential to Christian love (15 : 1-6) and which also produces (5 : 3-4) and maintains (15 : 4) hope. We Christians who, "by steadfastness," persevere in our love toward one another so that the salvific will of God is accomplished for the community (15 : 2), *thereby* maintain our "hope" of sharing in the future and final completion of God's salvation (15 : 4).

Coupled with "steadfastness" is "the encouragement of the scriptures" (15 : 4). As we have seen, *paraklēsis* expresses both "encouragement" and "comfort" or "consolation". That the will of God was accomplished through the love of Christ in enduring the reproaches of men for the sake of God (15 : 3) gives us the encouragement and comfort that the will of God for the good of the community will likewise be accomplished through our love toward one another (15 : 1-2). As it gives encouragement and comfort in the midst of daily Christian living, then, the *paraklēsis* that arises from God's scriptural word helps us keep and maintain our hope for God's future (15 : 4).

Paul bolsters his exhortation with a personal prayer-wish.[17] He prays that God may give the Roman Christians the steadfastness and encouragement they need "to think in the same way with one another, according to Christ Jesus" (15 : 5), that is, to exercise the love to which Paul has just exhorted them: They are not to "please" themselves (15 : 1) but to "please" their neighbor (15 : 2), as Christ did not "please" himself (15 : 3).[18] The result will be a unified Christian community, "so that together with one voice you may glorify the God and Father of our Lord Jesus Christ" (15 : 6). This very unity, in itself, as an accomplishment of God's will for the community, "glorifies" God. This unity that comes from a steadfast exercise of Christian love is thus a pre-condition for the community's liturgical praising

---

[16] For this meaning of *echomen* here, see Michel, *Römer*, 446; Cranfield, *Romans*, 735; Käsemann, *Romans*, 383; Wilckens, *Römer*, 3. 102.

[17] See G. P. Wiles, *Paul's Intercessory Prayers. The Significance of the Intercessory Prayer Passages in the Letters of St. Paul* (SNTSMS 24; Cambridge: Cambridge University Press, 1974) 79-83.

[18] "Thinking the same toward one another" is also part of genuine Christian love in 12 : 16.

and "glorifying" of God. And if we can "glorify" God in and through the exercise of the love that unifies us (15 : 5-6), then we are *thereby* maintaining our hope for the future and final "glory" of God (15 : 4; see 5:2).

A consideration of the significance of "glorify" illuminates the close relation between "glorifying God" and "maintaining hope". "To glorify" God means not only to "praise" him but to actually bring about the "glory" of God so that it becomes a reality in and through the act of "glorifying". When Christians "glorify" God, the "glory of God" is thus promoted or actualized through them. When the Roman Christians "glorify God" in and through their exercise of love, so that the will of God is being done for the community, they are thereby bringing about and promoting the "glory of God". We have already seen that the future "glory of God" is the goal of our hope (5 : 2 b; 8 : 18.24-25), so that the relation between "glorifying God" and "maintaining hope" now becomes clearer. By glorifying God in and through our exercise of love, we allow the glory of God to be accomplished through our daily Christian living, so that we may maintain the hope of likewise participating in the future and final "glory of God".

4. *By loving one another we may all abound in hope: Rom 15 : 7-13*

Paul's exhortation moves beyond the rift between the "strong" and the "weak" to the more general situation of the Christian community as composed of Jews and Gentiles.[19] He urges them to welcome one another because[20] Christ welcomed them "for the glory of God" (15 : 7). Paul earlier exhorted the Roman Christians to love one another in accord with Christ Jesus (15 : 3, 5) that they may "glorify God" (15 : 6), that is, further the "glory of God," and thereby "have" or maintain hope (15 : 4). Likewise, he now urges them to exercise love by welcoming one another to further the "glory of God". So, by welcoming one another "for the glory of God," the future goal of their hope (5 : 2 b; 8 : 18.24-25), Jewish and Gentile Christians may thereby maintain their hope.

Paul continues by solemnly declaring that Christ became a servant of the "circumcision," that is, of the Jews, "for the sake of God's fidelity" (15 : 8 a).

---

[19] Although the "strong" may be primarily Gentiles and the "weak" primarily Jewish Christians, the Jewish/Gentile situation here transcends the strong/weak problem; see Schlier, *Römerbrief,* 423.

[20] *Kathōs,* "as," "for," has more of a causal than a strictly comparative sense here; see Cranfield, *Romans,* 739; Schlier, *Römerbrief,* 423; Käsemann, *Romans,* 385.

The "fidelity," "faithfulness" or "trustworthiness" of God closely resonates with "the glory of God," so that "for the sake of God's fidelity" means ultimately "for the glory of God" (15 : 7b). [21]   And Christ became a servant of the Jews for the sake of God's fidelity precisely "to confirm the promises of the fathers" (15 : 8 b).   Being a Jew Christ not only "fulfilled" the promises that the Messiah would come from the Jews (see 1 : 2-3; 9 : 5; 15 : 12), but he also thereby "confirmed" or "made valid" the yet-to-be-fulfilled "promises of the fathers" for God's future salvation. [22]   In other words, by becoming a servant of the Jews Christ made possible the future fulfillment of the promises made to the Jewish patriarchs, so that these promises serve as a presently valid basis of hope for the future salvation of God. [23]

But Christ became a servant of the Jews also that "the Gentiles might glorify God for the sake of mercy" (15 : 9 a). [24]   That Christ has made the promises valid "for the sake of God's fidelity" to the Jews means that now the Gentiles can "glorify" God "for the sake of mercy". [25]   Thus, Christ "welcomed" both the Jews and the Gentiles among the Roman Christians, so that both play an essential role in "glorifying God" by "welcoming" one another in love for the sake of God's glory (15 : 7), the future goal of their hope.

That there can and must be a mutual love between Jews and Gentiles for the glory of God Paul illustrates by a series of scriptural quotations (15 : 9 b-12) linked together by a repetition of the word "Gentiles" and by various illustrations of "glorifying" God.   Whereas the first quotation (Ps 18 : 49) expresses primarily the Jewish praise of God among the Gentiles (15 : 9 b), the second quotation (Deut 32 : 43) addresses the Gentiles and invites them to rejoice along with God's people, Israel (15 : 10).   The third quotation (Ps 117 : 1) extends the invitation to "*all* the Gentiles" and to "*all*

---

[21] Note Rom 3 : 7 a: "But if through my falsehood the fidelity of God abounds to His glory..."

[22] Note Rom 9 : 4-5 a: "They are Israelites, and to them belong the sonship, the glory, the covenants, the giving of the Law, the worship, and the promises; to them belong the fathers, and from them is the Christ, according to the flesh." See also 3 : 1-2; 4 : 13-25.

[23] We have already seen in the case of Abraham (4 : 13-25) how the "promise" of God stimulates hope for the future.

[24] We take 15 : 9 a to be grammatically dependent upon *eis to* in 15 : 8 b; see Schlier, *Römerbrief,* 424.   For a discussion of the problem and other opinions, see Cranfield, *Romans,* 742-744; Käsemann, *Romans,* 385; Wilckens, *Römer,* 3. 106.

[25] *Alētheia* (fidelity) and *eleos* (mercy) are often linked together in the OT as a unity to describe God's salvific dealings on behalf of his people and thus serve to illustrate the unity and mutuality of Jews and Gentiles here.   For God's "mercy" toward the Gentiles, see 9 : 15.16.23; 11 : 31-32. See also Schlier, *Römerbrief,* 424 n. 7; Michel, *Römer,* 448 n. 25.

the peoples" to praise the Lord, the God of Israel (15 : 11). These scriptural promises invite the praise of God and exemplify how the Gentiles "glorify" God for the sake of mercy (15 : 9 a). They include both the Jewish (15 : 9 b-10) and the Gentile Christians (15 : 10-11) in the universal praising and glorifying of God. These exciting scriptural invitations thus encouragingly exhort the Roman Christians to welcome one another as part of Christian love (15 : 7). And they aptly illustrate "the encouragement of the scriptures" through which Christians maintain hope (15 : 4) by their love toward one another.

The fourth and final quotation (Isa 11 : 10) expresses the prophetic promise that the "sprout of Jesse," the Messiah, will come from the Jews and rule over the Gentiles, so that in him the Gentiles "will hope" (*elpiousin*) (15 : 12). This climax to the series of scriptural quotes most explicitly illustrates how Christ has fulfilled and confirmed the "promises of the fathers" (15 : 8), so that they are now a valid basis of hope for Christians. Having become a servant of the Jews (15 : 8) Christ has fulfilled the promise for a "sprout of Jesse," a Jewish Messiah, who would also rule the Gentiles. Christ has thus "confirmed" this promise as a valid basis of hope, so that its promise that the Gentiles "will hope" in him may now be fulfilled by the Roman Christians "welcoming" one another in love (15 : 7). As we have seen, Paul urges the Romans to the mutual exercise of Christian love (15 : 1-12) precisely so that they may have and maintain hope (15 : 4). The unity, harmony and mutual respect of the Christian community establishes, preserves and assures their hope for the future of God.

Paul climactically reinforces and sums up his preceding parenesis with a prayer for its fulfillment: "May the God of *hope* (*elpidos*) fill you with complete joy and peace in believing, so that you may abound in *hope* (*elpidi*) by the power of the Holy Spirit!" Paul addresses God as the "God of hope," that is, as the ultimate source and giver of hope. He prays that the God who gives hope may fill the Romans with complete "joy" and "peace" in believing. "Joy" characterizes the "glorifying" of God that is described in terms of rejoicing and praising in the scriptural citations of 15 : 9 b-11, and that is the result of Christians loving one another. And "peace" refers to the unity and harmony (15 : 6) that results from Christian love. This joy and peace with which the God of hope fills Christians when they love one another results in an increase and growth of hope so that their hope "abounds" or "overflows" (see 5 : 15, 17). And this superabundance of hope takes place through the power of the Holy Spirit, whose essential role for hope we have already seen (5 : 5; 8 : 23-27). Hence, in Paul's view, we can never have enough hope. Christian hope never stagnates; it can and must continually grow so that it "abounds".

C. Summary

Hope serves as an essential motivation in Paul's parenesis to a specific (14 : 1 – 15 : 13) as well as to the more general situation of daily Christian living (12 : 1 – 13 : 14). Maintaining the peace, unity and harmony of the community by loving one another, based upon Christ's love, allows us not only to keep and preserve hope but to abound in hope for God's future. Our consideration of Paul's parenesis, then, yields several points pertinent to our theme of hope in Romans: 1) Not only our present situation of hope (12 : 1-2) but also our ever approaching future hope (13 : 11-14) urgently motivates us to live in love of one another (13 : 8-10). 2) The different charisms in the Christian community should be exercised in love to preserve and promote hope (12 : 3-8). 3) Christians should submit to governing authorities (13 : 1-7) and not take revenge on enemies (12 : 17-21) nor judge one another (14 : 1-12) for the sake of their future hope in God. 4) Christians must not destroy the hope of others by their own convictions (14 : 13-23). 5) "Steadfastness" in suffering and constancy in prayer (12 : 12) are not only part of hope but also of love, so that Christians are to love one another with persevering steadfastness to maintain their hope for the future of God (12 : 9-16; 15 : 4-5). 6) The scriptures give Christians an attitude of "encouragement" and "comfort" so that they are able to love one another as Christ loved them (15 : 3.7) and thus maintain their hope (15 : 4-6.9 b-12). 7) When Christians love one another by steadfastness and encouragement, they "glorify God," (15 : 6), thus promoting the "glory of God," and thereby maintain their hope for the future and final "glory of God" (15 : 4-6.7-12). 8) Christians are to love one another that God may fill them with complete joy (12 : 12) and peace (14 : 17-19) so that their hope may increase and abound (15 : 13). Christian love, then, not only maintains hope but enables it to increase and grow. 9) God is a God of "steadfastness," "encouragement" (15 : 6) and "hope" (15 : 13). God himself gives the steadfastness and encouragement that establishes and preserves hope (15 : 4); and it is God who causes our hope to increase and overflow (15 : 13).

To sum up, in Rom 12 : 1 – 15 : 13, we may say that Paul has continued to encourage and awaken the hope of his readers (see 1 : 11-12). In Rom 1 – 8 Paul confidently proclaimed and demonstrated the absolutely assured hope that Christians may have for the future glory and salvation of God (see esp. 5 : 1-11; 8 : 18-39). In Rom 9 – 11 Paul increased this hope as he broadened its horizon to include the hope that *all* Israel will be saved (11 : 26 a), so that we may confidently hope in God's merciful salvation of *all* (11 : 32). And in Rom 12 : 1 – 15 : 13 Paul has applied the hope he previously proclaimed and demonstrated in Rom 1 – 11 to daily and critical situations of Christian living. He exhorts us to live out the hope that is ours by loving one another in order not only to maintain but to abundantly increase our hope for the future and final salvation of God.   When we read the prayer of Paul (15 : 13), which climaxes the entire letter's theological demonstration, in conjunction with Paul's stated intention of encouraging his readers to share the hope based on faith (1 : 11-12), it aptly sums up the entire theme of hope running throughout the letter: "May the God of *hope* fill you with complete joy and peace in believing, so that you may abound in *hope* by the power of the Holy Spirit!"

CHAPTER VII

Spreading the Gospel and Increasing Hope: Rom 15 : 14 – 16 : 27

In accord with our procedure we will consider this last section of the letter exclusively in terms of our theme of hope. Having completed his presentation of the gospel of hope (1 : 16 – 15 : 13), Paul concludes the letter by returning to the theme of his "apostolic hope" of spreading the gospel to all nations (15 : 14-21) (see 1 : 5.13-15).[1] The presentation of the gospel in the letter itself is meant to fulfill Paul's apostolic hope (1 : 14-15) of strengthening and encouraging the Christian hope of the Romans (1 : 11-12), who already believe in the gospel (1 . 8). In concluding the letter Paul explains the important role the Roman Christians play in his apostolic hope for the future (15 : 22-33). Paul's closing personal greetings to those he knows in Rome are thus related to his apostolic hope (16 : 1-16). A final exhortation involving the hope of the Roman community is included (16 : 17-20). And the closing doxology (16 : 25-27) aptly sums up the entire structure of hope presented in the letter.

A. Paul's Apostolic Hope of Spreading the Gospel of Hope: Rom 15 : 14-21

Since the faith of the Roman Christians is world renown (1 : 8 b), Paul is convinced that they are fully capable of advising themselves (15 : 14). Nevertheless, Paul has rather "boldly" written this letter to "remind" them of the gospel in which they believe, because God has bestowed upon Paul the grace to be a "minister" of Christ Jesus to all the nations in the "priestly service" of the gospel of God, so that the nations, by coming to faith in the gospel, may become an "offering" which is acceptable and consecrated by the Holy Spirit (15 : 15-16). In other words, Paul is obligated to present the gospel even to the Romans, who already believe in it (1 : 8), as part of his general apostolic hope of spreading the gospel of God to all nations (1 : 14-15). Because the Romans already have faith, Paul's presentation of the gospel within the letter (1 : 16 – 15 : 13) functions as a "reminder" (15 : 15) to

---

[1] For more on Paul's "apostolic hope," see Chapter II.

them—especially that they may have the "strength" and "encouragement" (1 : 11-12), that is, the hope, that comes from their faith.

Paul expresses his apostolic hope in terms of the "boasting before God" [2] that he has in Christ Jesus (15 : 17). This apostolic "boasting" emerges from what the risen Christ has already "accomplished" through Paul in word and deed in his ministry of spreading the gospel; and the future goal of this apostolic hope is the "obedience" of faith (see 1 : 5) among all the nations (15 : 18). Paul is thus drawing the Romans into his apostolic hope as he shares with them how the "power" of God's Spirit has enabled him to spread the gospel of Christ to its "full completion," to have its full salvific effect, throughout the entire eastern Mediterranean region—from Jerusalem and as far round as Illyricum (15 : 19). What God's power has already accomplished through Paul, then, increases his apostolic hope for the future spreading of the gospel. He ambitiously aspires to evangelize not where Christ has already been made known, so as not to build on someone else's foundation, but rather to evangelize those who have not yet heard about Christ so that they may come to believe by "seeing" and "understanding" (15 : 20-21). Paul's apostolic hope for the future is that the promise of Isa 52 : 15 be fulfilled through him: "Those who have never been told of him *will see*, and those who have never heard *will understand*." Paul now communicates and shares his "apostolic hope" with the Romans, since they are to significantly contribute to it.

B. The Role of the Roman Christians in Paul's Apostolic Hope: Rom 15 : 22-33

Paul's apostolic task of continually spreading the gospel through God's power to those who have not yet heard of Christ (15 : 17-21) has many times prevented him from fulfilling his "longing" to come in person to Rome (15 : 22; see 1 : 10-11.13). Although Paul has presented the gospel in his letter (see 1 : 15-16) as a substitute for his personal presence, now that he has finished his apostolic task "in these regions" from Jerusalem to Illyricum (15 : 19), he still has the "longing" (*epipothian*, see also 1 : 11) to come in person to the Romans and "hopes" (*elpizō*) to see them on his way to spreading the gospel to Spain (15 : 23-24). Paul has reached a turning point in his apostolic ministry: His success through the power of God in the eastern Mediterranean has provoked his hope of bringing the gospel to Spain. And the Christian community at Rome can contribute to this apostolic hope when Paul succeeds in visiting them by helping him on his journey to Spain

---

[2] We have already seen how "boasting before God" expresses hope in Romans: 2 : 17.23; 3 : 27; 4 : 2; 5 : 2.3.11.

with material support (food, money, companions)[3] after he has been spiritual-ly "satisfied" by them for a while (15 : 24), that is, "mutually encouraged" with them in the hope they share because of their common faith (see 1 : 11-12).[4]   Whereas Paul has written the letter (1 : 16– 15 : 13) with the intention of "strengthening" and "encouraging" (1 : 11-12) the Romans by proclaiming the hope they may have through their faith in the gospel, in his future visit with them, it is the Romans who can support, encourage and increase Paul's apostolic hope of spreading the gospel to Spain.   Thus will Paul and the Romans be "*mutually* encouraged" (1 : 12)—by the letter and by the visit. Paul's hope of visiting the Romans, then, is oriented to his hope of reaching Spain with the gospel.

But before Paul can fulfill his apostolic hope of going to Spain by way of his visit to Rome, he must fulfill another part of his apostolic hope—that of delivering the contribution of Macedonia and Achaia to the poor in Jerusal-em (15 : 25-26).   The Jerusalem community holds a special significance with regard to the gospel of hope.   Paul has already shown how the Gentiles share in the "spiritual blessings" (15 : 27) that have originated from Jerusalem, that is, in the gospel of hope based on the promises given Israel (see 1 : 1-2; 3 : 2; 9 - 11; 15 : 7-12).   The hope the Gentiles now have is founded on their faith in the gospel which originated from Jerusalem, so that the Gentiles are all the more indebted to serve the Jerusalem community in "material blessings" (15 : 27).   Once Paul has completed this necessary apostolic task and assured that the contribution to Jerusalem has been successfully delivered and offi-cially received, he hopes to go on by way of the Romans to Spain (15 : 28). And the completion of his apostolic ministry in Jerusalem will give Paul the confident hope of knowing that when he comes to Rome he will come in the fullness of the blessing of Christ (15 : 29).   Paul's ministry to Jerusalem will thus benefit those in Rome, as it will enable him to bring them the full blessing of Christ.

But as the Roman Christians play an important role in Paul's apostolic hope for Spain (15 : 24), so they must also assist him in his apostolic hope for Jerusalem.   Paul urgently exhorts the Roman brethren to share in his hope for the success of the Jerusalem ministry by praying before God on his behalf.   They are to join in his hope by striving together with him as they actualize their hope in their prayers:[5]   "I exhort you, brothers, through our

---

[3] BAGD, 709.

[4] Schlier, *Römerbrief,* 435; Wilckens, *Römer,* 3. 124; M. Kettunen, *Der Abfas-sungszweck des Römerbriefes* (Annales Academiae Scientiarum Fennicae Dissertationes Humanarum Litterarum 18; Helsinki: Suomalainene Tiedeakatemia, 1979) 163-164.

[5] Prayer, which is oriented to the future completion of God's salvific plan, the future goal of hope, can be considered "hope in action" or an "actualization" of the attitude of hope; see 8 : 26-27; 12 : 12.

Lord Jesus Christ and through the love inspired by the Spirit, to strive together with me in your prayers to God on my behalf" (15 : 30). The Romans are to pray that God accomplish his salvific will on Paul's behalf in Jerusalem and rescue Paul from the unbelievers in Judea so that his service to Jerusalem be rendered acceptable to the saints (15 : 31). Then, Paul can fulfill, through the will of God, his apostolic hope of visiting the Romans in joy and being "refreshed" together with them, that is, of being "mutually encouraged" in their mutual hope (15 : 32; see 1 : 11-12; 15 : 24). Paul closes his exhortation with the prayer that the God who gives peace may be with all of the Christians in Rome (15 : 33).

C. Paul Greets Contributors of His Apostolic Hope: Rom 16 : 1-16

Many of those whom Paul recommends the Roman community to greet have played significant roles in Paul's past apostolic ministry.[6] They serve as testimony to his success in bringing the gospel to its full completion in the regions from Jerusalem to Illyricum (15 : 17-19). They have shared in Paul's apostolic hope of bringing all nations to the "obedience of faith" (1 : 5; 15 : 18) in the gospel that gives hope. They serve as a further basis, then, for Paul's apostolic hope with regard to Spain (15 : 22-33). And by recommending them to the other Roman Christians whom he does not yet know Paul draws the entire Roman community together to share in his apostolic hope for the future. Those who have worked with Paul to spread and increase this apostolic hope are the following:

First of all, Paul recommends to them Phoebe, "our sister," a deaconess of service to the church in Cenchreae (16 : 1); they are to assist her in whatever she needs, because she has been a helper of many including Paul himself

---

[6] There has been considerable discussion about whether chapter 16 belongs to the original letter, but a number of recent interpreters tend to accept it. See W.-H. Ollrog, "Die Abfassungsverhältnisse von Röm 16," *Kirche* (Festschrift für G. Bornkamm zum 75. Geburtstag; ed. D. Lührmann and G. Strecker; Tübingen: Mohr, 1980) 221 n. 3, for a list of those who argue that Rom 16 belongs to Rom 1-15, to which may be added: H. Gamble, *The Textual History of the Letter to the Romans* (Studies and Documents 42; Grand Rapids: Eerdmans, 1977). We accept the conclusion of both Ollrog and Gamble that Rom 16 can be fully understood as the original conclusion of the letter to the Romans. According to Ollrog ("Abfassungsverhältnisse," 227, 230-232), Rom 16 : 17-20 may be a later interpolation; Gamble (*Textual History*, 52-53), however, thinks even these verses need not be secondary. There is a consensus among scholars that Rom 16 : 25-27 are a later addition.

(16 : 2).[7] Prisca and Aquila have been "fellow-workers"[8] of Paul in his apostolate (16 : 3), even to the point of risking their own lives for Paul, so that he
along with all the churches of the Gentiles thank them (16 : 4).[9] Epaenetus
was the "first-fruit" of missionary success, the first convert for Christ in Asia
(16 : 5). Mary has "labored" hard in apostolic work on behalf of the Romans (16 : 6). Andronicus and Junias were closely related to Paul in his
apostolate as his "kinsmen" and "fellow-prisoners," who are notable among
the apostles and who were in Christ before Paul (16 : 7). Ampliatus is Paul's
"beloved" in the Lord (16 : 8), an expression of an especially close relationship to Paul. Urbanus is another "fellow-worker," Stachys "my beloved"
(16 : 9) and Herodion "my kinsman" (16 : 11). Tryphaena and Tryphosa
were missionary "workers" with Paul in the Lord; and the beloved Persis
has likewise "labored" hard for the apostolate in the Lord (16 : 12). And
after recommending several more of his close associates (16 : 13-15) Paul concludes this set of greetings: "Greet one another with a holy kiss. All the
churches of Christ greet you" (16 : 16).

D. A Final Exhortation of Hope: Rom 16 : 17-20

Even if it comes from a later interpolator, the final exhortation in
16 : 17-20 expresses a hope conforming to that which occurs throughout the
rest of the letter.[10] Paul or an interpolator warns the Roman brethren to
avoid those enemies of the community who create dissensions and difficulties
in opposition to the teaching, the gospel of hope, that they have learned
(16 : 17; and see 6 : 17). Such persons do not live in accord with Christian
hope, for they do not "serve" (see 6 : 15-23; 14 : 7-9) our Lord Christ but
themselves, and by fair and flattering words deceive the hearts of the unsus-
pecting (16 : 18). The author is here exhorting the Roman Christians to
maintain and live in accord with their hope: Their "obedience" of faith (see
1 : 5; 10 : 16), the grounds for their hope, has become known to all (see 1 : 8;
15 : 14), so that the author rejoices over them but wants them to maintain
the hope based on this faith by being "wise" as to what is good, and "inno-
cent as to what is evil" (16 : 19). The "good" refers to the accomplishment

---

[7] W.-H. Ollrog, *Paulus und seine Mitarbeiter. Untersuchungen zu Theorie und
Praxis der paulinischen Mission* (WMANT 50; Neukirchen-Vluyn: Neukirchener Verlag, 1979) 31.

[8] Ibid., 63-72.

[9] Ibid., 24-27.

[10] On 16 : 17-20, see, in addition to the commentaries, Kettunen, *Abfassungszweck,*
62-73. Ollrog ("Abfassungsverhältnisse," 233-234) thinks it possible that 16 : 17-20
was added about 96 A.D. at the time that 1 Clement quoted from Romans.

8

of God's "good" salvific will, the future goal of hope (8 : 28), according to which Paul has already exhorted the Roman Christians to live in order to maintain their hope (see 12 : 1-2.9.17.21; 13 : 3-4; 14 : 16; 15 : 2). The future eschatological hope that the "God of peace will soon crush Satan under your feet" (16 : 20 a) provides the climactic motivation for the exhortation.

E. Final Greetings and Doxology: Rom 16 : 21-27

The final greetings (16 : 21-23) emanate from some more of those who have been closely related to Paul in his apostolic hope of spreading the gospel: Timothy is "my fellow-worker," and Lucius, Jason and Sosipater are "my kinsmen" (16 : 21). Tertius wrote the letter (16 : 22), Gaius was a "host" to Paul and Erastus the "treasurer" of the city (16 : 23).

Whether or not the doxology in 16 : 25-27 belonged to the original letter and whether or not it was composed by Paul,[11] it contains the entire structure of hope as presented in the letter. The doxology gives glory to the uniquely "wise" God who gives the hope that has now become available through faith in the gospel. It begins by addressing God as he who has the "power" to "strengthen" Christians in accord with the gospel, the preaching of Jesus Christ (16 : 25 a). This aptly sums up Paul's purpose of presenting the gospel of hope in the letter to the Romans (1 : 15-16) in order that they may be spiritually "strengthened" (1 : 11) and "encouraged" (1 : 12) in the hope that comes from their faith. This spiritual "strength," an attribute of hope (see 4 : 18-20) has its firm foundation in the gospel, which, as the decisive revelation of the mystery kept secret for long ages but now disclosed and made known through the prophetic writings (see 1 : 1-2; 3 : 21), according to the command of God (16 : 25 b-26), fulfills past hopes and awakens new hope. The gospel likewise incites the apostolic hope whose future goal is the "obedience of faith among all nations" (16 : 26 b; see 1 : 5). The doxology, then, praises God for the spiritual "strength," the hope, that comes from faith in the gospel, the gospel which also awakens the apostolic hope of bringing about the "obedience of faith" among all nations. And by giving "glory" to God the doxology is itself an actualization of the attitude of hope (see 15 : 5-13).

---

[11] In addition to the commentaries, see J. K. Elliott, "The Language and Style of the Concluding Doxology to the Epistle to the Romans," *ZNW* 72 (1981) 124-130. He does not think that 16 : 25-27 is from Paul. And Ollrog ("Abfassungsverhältnisse," 227), following the consensus among scholars on this point, thinks it very probable that 16 : 25-27 is a later addition.

F. Summary

With regard to our theme of hope in this section of Romans (15 : 14 – 16 : 27) we may list the following results:

1) With the Roman Christians who already exhibit the "obedience of faith" (1 : 5.8; 15 : 14) Paul shares his apostolic hope of evangelizing where Christ has not yet been made known in order to bring about the "obedience of faith" among all the nations (15 : 14-21).

2) The Roman Christians play an important role within Paul's apostolic hope: He hopes to see them in person not only to be encouraged by them in their mutual hope based on their common faith (1 : 11-12; 15 : 24.32) but also to be supported by them in his apostolic hope to spread the gospel as far as Spain (15 : 22-24), after he has successfully completed his apostolic ministry of delivering the contribution of the Gentiles to Jerusalem through the help of the Roman Christians' prayers (15 : 25-33). In this way the Roman Christians not only share in but contribute to and promote the apostolic hope of spreading the gospel that gives hope.

3) There have been many "fellow-workers" of Paul in his apostolic hope who serve as evidence of the spreading of the gospel in the past (15 : 17-19) and provoke and increase the hope of spreading it in the future—as far as Spain (16 : 1-16.21-23).

4) The hope based on the well known faith of the Roman Christians motivates them to avoid the false teaching which threatens the community (16 : 17-20).

5) The concluding doxology fittingly sums up the hope of the letter to the Romans: it is itself an actualization of confident hope in the God who can spiritually strengthen Christians in their hope based on the gospel, the gospel which arouses the apostolic hope for the "obedience of the faith" which will extend hope to all (16 : 25-27).

CHAPTER VIII

Conclusion: Romans—Paul's Letter of Hope

Our investigation of the theme of hope in Romans has yielded results not only for Paul's theology of hope but for his letter to the Romans. With regard to method, we have attempted to demonstrate the appropriateness of considering all of the various aspects to the dynamics of hope operative throughout the entire letter in order to gain a complete appreciation for the significance of Christian hope as Paul proclaims it. And a consideration of hope throughout the entire letter contributes an insight into the letter's over-all unity and coherence. The letter as a whole makes a concerted effort to awaken and increase the hope of its readers; from beginning to end its over-all tone is that of hopefulness, so that the letter to the Romans can truly be called Paul's "letter of hope".

Without repeating the results from the summaries which conclude the preceding chapters, we briefly list what we consider to be the major points made by our study of the hope of Paul's letter to the Romans:

1) Even the introductory (1 : 1-15) and concluding sections (15 : 14 – 16 : 27) which "frame" Paul's presentation of the gospel in the more properly didactic and demonstrative portion of the letter (1 : 16 – 15 : 13) concern hope. The letter literally begins and ends on the note of hope. The gospel "promised beforehand" (1 : 2) not only imparts to all Christians the "strength" and "encouragement" (1 : 11-12) of hope but also induces Paul's apostolic hope of spreading this gospel of Christian hope to all (1 : 5.13-15; 15 : 17-21).

2) Before Paul proclaims and demonstrates our new Christian hope (3 : 21-31; 5 : 1-11), he indicates the great need for hope by first explaining former hopelessness (1 : 18-32) and presumption (2 : 1 – 3 : 8). The universal extent and power of sinfulness has brought about a situation of total hopelessness for all (3 : 9-20)—"for *all* have sinned and lack the glory of God" (3 : 23). Thus, it is necessary to first recognize and understand the full extent of hopelessness before one can fully understand and appreciate the new situation of Christian hope.

3) Even when Paul begins to explain our new Christian hope (5 : 12 – 7 : 25), he does so against the background of our previous hopelessness. Our new hope must be lived out now lest we fall back into hopelessness under the powers of sin, death and the Law (6 : 1 – 7 : 25). Christian hope, then, is entirely realistic as it takes into full account the ever-present

threat of hopelessness. Christians can and must live now the hope they possess and proclaim.

4) In Romans Paul's description of the general and fundamental attitude of our Christian "hope" is not limited to his use of the word *elpis* but includes a number of various other expressions, such as: "not being shamed" (by God), "boasting before God," joy, confident certainty about the future, patient and steadfast endurance, eager expectation for God's future glory, peace with God and one another, perseverance in prayer, etc. These various expressions of hope center around our confident certainty that "we will be saved" (5 : 9-10), which is not merely a wishful thinking but is firmly grounded in the great love God has manifested for us in Christ (5 : 1-11; 8 : 31-39). This overwhelming confidence and certainty of our Christian hope realistically reckons with ever-present sufferings and obstacles to hope. It is a vigorous, vibrant hope in the midst of sufferings which are "against hope" (see 4 : 18-25; 5 : 3-4; 8 : 17-39). But rather than destroying or dampening our hope, sufferings increase and thus strengthen our hope (5 : 3-4). Christian hope for God's future triumph over present sufferings is thus absolutely assured (8 : 31-39).

5) The hope that "all Israel will be saved" (11 : 26 a) and that God "will have mercy on all" (11 : 32) in Rom 9 – 11 complements the confident certainty of Christian hope expressed in Rom 1 – 8: The hope of Rom 9 – 11 assures that our Christian hope remains authentic by keeping it radically open to the uncontrollable and incalculable future salvation of God (11 : 33-36). And the inclusion of Rom 9 – 11 in our investigation further indicates the letter's unity and coherence in making a concerted effort to arouse hope in its readers.

6) The long-recognized relationship between Christian "hope" and "love" (*agapē*), the "ethical" dimension of hope, we have confirmed and made more precise by including Rom 12 : 1 – 15 : 13 in our study: Christian hope can and must be "lived" now in and through an active care and concern, a Christian "love," for one another. There exists a close interrelationship between Christian hope and love: we manifest our present hope by our love and love "maintains" our hope for the future of God (15 : 4). Christian hope, then, can not remain static or stagnant; the steadfastness of love not only maintains hope but causes it to grow and increase to abundance. Paul's prayer in 15 : 13 aptly sums up this dynamic hope of Christians: "May the God of hope fill you with complete joy and peace in believing, so that you may *abound* in hope by the power of the Holy Spirit!"

Bibliography

I. Abbreviations of Reference Works

APOT R. H. Charles (ed.), *Apocrypha and Pseudepigrapha of the Old Testament*
BAGD W. Bauer, W. F. Arndt, F. W. Gingrich and F. W. Danker, *Greek–English Lexicon of the NT*
BDF F. Blass, A. Debrunner and R. W. Funk, *A Greek Grammar of the NT*
Str–B (H. Strack and) P. Billerbeck, *Kommentar zum Neuen Testament*

II. Literature

Balz, H. R. *Heilsvertrauen und Welterfahrung. Strukturen der paulinischen Eschatologie nach Römer 8,18-39.* BEvT 59. Munich: Kaiser, 1971.
Barrett, C. K. *A Commentary on the Epistle to the Romans.* HNTC. New York: Harper & Row, 1957.
Bauer, J. B. "Hope." *Sacramentum Verbi.* 1st vol. New York: Herder and Herder, 1970, 376-379.
Bauernfeind, O. "*mataios.*" *TDNT* 4 (1967) 519-524.
———. "*nikaō.*" *TDNT* 4 (1967) 942-945.
Behm, J. "*kardia.*" *TDNT* 3 (1965) 608-614.
Berger, K. "Abraham in den paulinischen Hauptbriefen." *MTZ* 17 (1966) 47-89.
Bertram, G. "*Apokaradokia.*" *ZNW* 49 (1958) 264-270.
———. "*phrēn.*" *TDNT* 9 (1974) 220-235.
———. "*ōdin.*" *TDNT* 9 (1974) 667-674.
Black, M. *Romans.* NCB. London: Oliphants, 1973.
Büchsel, F. "*allassō.*" *TDNT* 1 (1964) 251-259.
———. "*bastazō.*" *TDNT* 1 (1964) 596.
Bultmann, R. "*aischynō.*" *TDNT* 1 (1964) 189-191.
———. "*thanatos.*" *TDNT* 3 (1965) 7-25.
Byrne, B. *'Sons of God'–'Seed of Abraham'.* AnBib 83. Rome: Biblical Institute, 1979.
Cazelles, H. "A propos de quelques textes difficiles relatifs à la justice de Dieu dans l'Ancien Testament." *RB* 58 (1951) 169-188.
Conzelmann, H. "Hoffnung im NT." *RGG* 3 (1959) 417-418.
Cranfield, C. E. B. *A Critical and Exegetical Commentary on the Epistle to the Romans.* ICC. 1st vol.: Introduction and Commentary on Romans I–VIII. 2 d vol.: Commentary on Romans IX–XVI and Essays. Edinburgh: T. & T. Clark, 1975, 1979.

Dabelstein, R. *Die Beurteilung der 'Heiden' bei Paulus.* Beiträge zur biblischen Exegese und Theologie 14. Frankfurt/Bern/Cirencester: Lang, 1981.

Dahl, N. A. *Studies in Paul.* Minneapolis: Augsburg, 1977.

Delling, G. *"apokaradokia."* *TDNT* 1 (1964) 393.

———. *"archō."* *TDNT* 1 (1964) 478-489.

———. *"plērophoreō."* *TDNT* 6 (1968) 309-310.

Denton, D. R. *"Apokaradokia."* *ZNW* 73 (1982) 138-140.

Dietzfelbinger, Ch. *Paulus und das Alte Testament. Die Hermeneutik des Paulus, untersucht an seiner Deutung der Gestalt Abrahams.* Theologische Existenz Heute 95. Munich: Kaiser, 1961.

Elliott, J. K. "The Language and Style of the Concluding Doxology to the Epistle to the Romans." *ZNW* 72 (1981) 124-130.

Fitzmyer, J. A. "Reconciliation in Pauline Theology." *To Advance the Gospel. New Testament Studies.* New York: Crossroad, 1981, 162-185.

Foerster, W. *"eirēnē."* *TDNT* 2 (1964) 400-402, 406-420.

———. *"echthros."* *TDNT* 2 (1964) 811-816.

———. *"klēronomos."* *TDNT* 3 (1965) 767-769, 776-785.

Gamble, H. *The Textual History of the Letter to the Romans.* Studies and Documents 42. Grand Rapids: Eerdmans, 1977.

Goppelt, L. "Apokalyptik und Typologie bei Paulus." *TLZ* 89 (1964) 321-344.

Grundmann, W. *"apekdechomai."* *TDNT* 2 (1964) 56.

———. *"dokimos."* *TDNT* 2 (1964) 255-260.

Hauck, F. *"makarios."* *TDNT* 4 (1967) 367-370.

———. *"hypomenō."* *TDNT* 4 (1967) 581-588.

Heidland, H. W. *"logizomai."* *TDNT* 4 (1967) 284-292.

Hoffmann, E. "Hoffnung." *Theologisches Begriffslexikon zum Neuen Testament.* 2 d vol. Wuppertal: Brockhaus, 1969, 722-728.

Hofius, O. "Eine altjüdische Parallele zu Röm. iv. 17 b." *NTS* 18 (1971-72) 93-94.

———. "Erwägungen zur Gestalt und Herkunft des paulinischen Versöhnungsgedankens." *ZTK* 77 (1980) 186-199.

———. "'Gott hat unter uns aufgerichtet das Wort der Versöhnung' (2 Kor 5.19)." *ZNW* 71 (1980) 3-20.

Jacob, E. "Abraham et sa signification pour la foi chrétienne." *RHPR* 42 (1962) 148-156.

Jeremias, Joachim. *"Abraam."* *TDNT* 1 (1964) 8-9.

———. *"polloi."* *TDNT* 6 (1968) 536-545.

Käsemann, E. "The Faith of Abraham in Romans 4." *Perspectives on Paul.* London: SCM, 1971, 79-101.

———. *Commentary on Romans.* Grand Rapids: Eerdmans, 1980.

Kerstiens, F. "Hope." *Sacramentum Mundi.* 3 d vol. New York: Herder and Herder, 1969, 61-65.

Kettunen, M. *Der Abfassungszweck des Römerbriefes.* Annales Academiae Scientiarum Fennicae Dissertationes Humanarum Litterarum 18. Helsinki: Suomalainen Tiedeakatemia, 1979.

Kittel, G. *"dokeō."* *TDNT* 2 (1964) 232-237, 242-255.

Kuss, O. *Der Römerbrief.* Erste Lieferung (Röm 1,1 bis 6,11). 2 d ed. Zweite Lieferung (Röm 6,11 bis 8,19). 2 d ed. Dritte Lieferung (Röm 8,19 bis 11,36). Regensburg: Pustet, 1963, 1963, 1978.

Lack, R. *La Symbolique du Livre d'Isaïe. Essai sur l'image littéraire comme élément de structuration.* AnBib 59. Rome: Biblical Institute, 1973.

Lambrecht, J. "Present World and Christian Hope. A Consideration of Rom. 8 : 18-30." *Jeevadhara* 8 (1978) 29-39.

Lausberg, H. *Handbuch der Literarischen Rhetorik.* 2 d ed. Munich: Hueber, 1973.

Loane, M. L. *The Hope of Glory. An Exposition of The Eighth Chapter in The Epistle to The Romans.* London: Hodder and Stoughton, 1968.

Lyonnet, S. "De "Iustitia Dei" in Epistola ad Romanos." *VD* 25 (1947) 23-34, 118-121, 129-144, 193-203, 257-263.

―――. "Note sur le plan de l'épître aux Romains." *RSR* 39 (1951) 301-316.

―――. "L'histoire du salut selon le chapitre VII de l'épître aux Romains." *Bib* 43 (1962) 117-151.

―――. "De notione "iustitiae Dei" apud S. Paulum." *VD* 42 (1964) 121-152.

―――. *Les étapes du mystère du Salut selon l'épître aux Romains.* Paris: Cerf, 1969.

―――. *Quaestiones in Epistulam ad Romanos. Series Altera. Rom 9-11.* 3 d ed. Rome: Biblical Institute, 1975.

Macquarrie, J. *Christian Hope.* New York: Seabury, 1978.

Maillot, A. *L'Epître aux Romains, épître de l'espérance. Essai sur le plan de l'Epître aux Romains.* BVC 84. Bruges: Desclée De Brouwer, 1968.

Mantey, J. R. "The Causal Use of *Eis* in the New Testament." *JBL* 70 (1951) 45-48.

Martin, R. P. *Reconciliation. A Study of Paul' Theology.* New Foundations Theological Library. Atlanta: Knox, 1981.

Mauerer, C. "Der Schluß "a minore ad majus" als Element paulinischer Theologie." *TLZ* 85 (1960) 149-152.

Mayer, G. "Aspekte des Abrahambildes in der hellenistisch-jüdischen Literatur." *EvT* 32 (1972) 118-127.

Menezes, F. "Christian Hope of Glory. Rom 8 : 18-30." *Biblebhashyam* 5 (1979) 208-225.

Metzger, B. M. *A Textual Commentary on the Greek New Testament.* London-New York: United Bible Societies, 1971.

Michel, O. *Der Brief an die Römer.* MeyerK 4. 14th ed. Göttingen: Vandenhoeck & Ruprecht, 1978.

Müller, H. "Der rabbinische Qal–Wachomer-Schluß in paulinischer Typologie." *ZNW* 58 (1967) 73-92.

Nebe, G. *'Hoffnung' bei Paulus. Elpis und ihre Synonyme im Zusammenhang der Eschatologie.* SUNT 16. Göttingen: Vandenhoeck & Ruprecht, 1983.

Oepke, A. *"eis."* TDNT 2 (1964) 420-434.

Ollrog, W.-H. *Paulus und seine Mitarbeiter. Untersuchungen zu Theorie und Praxis der paulinischen Mission.* WMANT 50. Neukirchen-Vluyn: Neukirchener Verlag, 1979.

―――. "Die Abfassungsverhältnisse von Röm 16." *Kirche.* Festschrift für G. Bornkamm zum 75. Geburtstag. Ed. D. Lührmann and G. Strecker. Tübingen: Mohr, 1980, 221-244.

Popkes, W. "Zum Aufbau und Charakter von Römer 1.18-32." *NTS* 28 (1982) 490-501.

de la Potterie, I. "*Charis* paulinienne et *charis* johannique." *Jesus und Paulus.*

Festschrift für W. G. Kümmel zum 70. Geburtstag. Ed. E. E. Ellis and E. Gräß-
    er. Göttingen: Vandenhoeck & Ruprecht, 1975, 256-282.
Rahner, K. "On the Theology of Hope." *Theological Investigations.* 10th vol. New
    York: Herder and Herder, 1973, 242-259.
Räisänen, H. "Das 'Gesetz des Glaubens' (Röm. 3.27) und das 'Gesetz des Geistes'
    (Röm. 8.2)." *NTS* 26 (1979-80) 101-117.
Rhyne, C. T. *Faith Establishes the Law.* SBLDS 55. Chico: Scholars Press, 1981.
Rische, J. H. "'Waiting in Hope': An Exegetical Study of Romans 8 : 19-22." A
    Research Paper Presented to Concordia Seminary, St. Louis, 1970.
Robinson, D. W. B. "The Priesthood of Paul in the Gospel of Hope." *Reconciliation
    and Hope. New Testament Essays on Atonement and Eschatology presented to
    L. L. Morris on his 60th Birthday.* Ed. R. Banks. Exeter: Paternoster, 1974,
    231-245.
Rolland, Ph. "'Il est notre justice, notre vie, notre salut'. L'ordonnance des thèmes
    majeurs de l'Epître aux Romains." *Bib* 56 (1975) 394-404.
――――. *Epître aux Romains. Texte grec structuré.* Rome: Biblical Institute, 1980.
Salom, A. P. "The Imperatival Use of the Participle in the NT." *AusBR* 11 (1963)
    41-49.
Schlier, H. "*thlibō.*" *TDNT* 3 (1965) 139-148.
――――. "On Hope." *The Relevance of the New Testament.* New York: Herder and
    Herder, 1968, 142-155.
――――. "Das, worauf alles wartet. Eine Auslegung von Römer 8,18-30." *Das Ende
    der Zeit. Exegetische Aufsätze und Vorträge III.* Freiburg/Basel/Wien: Herder,
    1971, 250-270.
――――. *Der Römerbrief.* HTKNT 6. Freiburg/Basel/Wien: Herder, 1977.
Schneider, J. "*stenazō.*" *TDNT* 7 (1971) 600-603.
Stählin, G. "*orgē.*" *TDNT* 5 (1967) 419-447.
Strack, H. L. *Einleitung in Talmud und Midrasch.* 6th ed. Munich: Beck, 1976.
Stuhlmacher, P. *Gerechtigkeit Gottes bei Paulus.* FRLANT 87. Göttingen: Vanden-
    hoeck & Ruprecht, 1965.
Sudbrack, J. "Der Hymnus auf die Hoffnung. Eine Einführung in das Verständnis
    von Röm 8, 19-39." *Geist und Leben* 41 (1968) 224-228.
Vallauri, E. "I gemiti dello Spirito Santo (Rom. 8,26 s.)." *RivB* 27 (1979) 95-113.
Wedderburn, A. J. M. "Romans 8.26—Towards a Theology of Glossolalia?" *SJT* 28
    (1975) 369-377.
Wilckens, U. *Der Brief an die Römer.* EKKNT 6/1-2-3. 1. Teilband Röm 1-5. 2.
    Teilband Röm 6-11. 3. Teilband Röm 12-16. Neukirchen-Vluyn: Neukirchen-
    er Verlag, 1978, 1980, 1982.
Wiles, G. P. *Paul's Intercessory Prayers. The Significance of the Intercessory Prayer
    Passages in the Letters of St. Paul.* SNTSMS 24. Cambridge: Cambridge Uni-
    versity Press, 1974.
Williams, S. K. "The "Righteousness of God" in Romans." *JBL* 99 (1980) 241-
    290
Wolter, M. *Rechtfertigung und zukünftiges Heil. Untersuchungen zu Röm 5,1-11.*
    BZNW 43. Berlin/New York: de Gruyter, 1978.
Woschitz, K. M. *Elpis–Hoffnung. Geschichte, Philosophie, Exegese, Theologie eines
    Schlüsselbegriffs.* Wien/Freiburg/Basel: Herder, 1979.

Zahn, T. *Der Brief des Paulus an die Römer*. KNT 6. 2 d ed. Leipzig: Deichert, 1910.

Zerwick, M. *Biblical Greek*. 4th ed. Rome: Biblical Institute, 1963.

————. "Drama populi Israel secundum Rom 9–11." *VD* 46 (1968) 321-338

Zerwick, M. and Grosvenor, M. *A Grammatical Analysis of the Greek New Testament*. 2 vols. Rome: Biblical Institute, 1974, 1979.

Zorell, F. *Lexicon Graecum Novi Testamenti*. 3 d ed. Paris: Lethielleux, 1961, reprinted, Rome: Biblical Institute, 1978.

INDEX OF SCRIPTURE REFERENCES

Finito di stampare nel mese di maggio 1987
SCUOLA TIPOGRAFICA S. PIO X – VIA DEGLI ETRUSCHI, 7 – ROMA